Be the
Elephant

Be the Elephant

Build a Bigger, *Better* Business

by Steve Kaplan

Workman Publishing, New York

Library of Congress Cataloging-in-Publication Data is available.

ISBN-13: 978-0-7611-4448-9
ISBN-10: 0-7611-4448-X

Workman books are available at special discounts when purchased in bulk for premiums and sales promotions as well as for fund-raising or educational use. Special editions or book excerpts also can be created to specification. For details, contact the Special Sales Director at the address below.

Design by Paul Gamarello
Photography by Steve Grubman

Author Steve Kaplan may be contacted at 312-822-3435
stevekaplan@differencemaker.com
www.differencemaker.com

Workman Publishing Company, Inc.
225 Varick Street
New York, NY 10014-4381
www.workman.com

Printed in U.S.A.
First printing December 2006

10 9 8 7 6 5 4 3 2 1

Dedication

*To every entrepreneur and salesperson, working endless
hours in pursuit of your dreams: Remember, success can be
right around the corner—keep your eyes open.*

To Andi: for your support and love.

To Ryan: You continue to make me proud every single day.

*To Madison (a.k.a. Mouse): Always follow your heart
and pursue your passions.*

*To my parents, Ila, Jerry, JB, Lourdes, Joe, and Ferne:
for your love and support through the years.*

*To Brendi and Nanci: Thank you for always being there
for me. I think we'll always be upstairs, getting ready
to go out, making fun of each other.*

*To my nieces and nephews, Alex, Samantha, Zach, Nicky,
Emily, Sean, and Meghan: Your time is coming.*

*To Paul, Jeff, Heidi, and Ross:
You guys round out the asylum.*

*To my friends, who have been in my life for so long:
Through all the crazy times, to years of playing sports,
careers and families, we've remained close and are always
there for each other during good times and bad.
You've made the ride more than amazing, and I love you all.*

Contents

Part V: Creating Value

Part VI: Killer Mistakes

Preface

It's Great to Be Gray

Who Are You?

- You're the owner of an e-commerce business. You've made it over the second-year hump and are poised to break out, but you're unsure about which strategy is best to grow your business. You don't have a ton of money, so you need to make the right growth decision the first time. One misstep will kill your momentum.
- You run a three-person gourmet cookie company with a few corporate customers that take up most of your time. With such a small customer and employee base, you're understandably nervous. You know that you need to grow, but how to start the process without upending your existing business? Implementing a growth strategy might upset your large customers, prompting them to move along to that next cookie. And you do not want to be left with crumbs.

- You're a sales professional, selling mortgages. You're doing pretty well and have great relationships with many of your clients. You know that if you had more things to sell them, it would be a cakewalk, but you're not sure how to develop new offerings, especially ones they will prepay for.
- You're the senior partner in a CPA firm. You've always been motivated by a desire to become the best CPA you can be. You want your work to matter, to be recognized for its quality and superiority. You're great at your job, but you've neglected the business end of your business, and your client base is shrinking. Now you see the need to grow, but the resources available to you don't offer an obvious path to growth.
- You own a $50 million consulting business. You've been cruising along, selling the same service for years. A few years back, you tried expanding your services into new markets, but the extra duties and responsibilities took your employees' attention away from your core clientele and the effort failed, almost costing you your business. You're doing okay now, but you don't want to work like a dog forever.
- You're a partner in a marketing firm that's been doing steady business for a few years. You're not growing, but that's all right, because you don't want the worries of a larger business. Besides, you wouldn't know what to do to get bigger. You're okay with the status quo for now. Yet you can't help being a little worried, because you've seen many other businesses like yours cruise along at treetop level for years and then crash and burn. All it took was a brief financial stumble, and the owners were unable to adapt or compensate.

Not-Growing Pains

If you can identify with any of these people, this book's for you. You realize that your business is living pretty close to the edge. You don't have much flexibility or reserve. Yes, you may be spared the giant problems of giant companies, but the anxieties and stresses of eking out profits and growth in your business, at its current size, are hardly a blessing. You're worried about Incredible Shrinking Business Syndrome. You also fret that you'll never make the big bucks you've dreamed of. But just *thinking* about growing gives you the jitters. Rock and a hard place.

Somewhere in the back of your mind, you remember what older, wiser capitalists have told you: In business, there's no standing still. Avoiding growth goes against the laws of nature; you're either growing or dying, yet finding a niche and managing to operate there happily ever after is riddled with risk. A recession, a new technology, even a miscalculation or a sudden illness can lead to a quick demise.

Okay, so "slow and steady" isn't as good a long-term growth strategy as you thought. You can see that a larger, broader-based business would give you more security in the long run, and that's your ultimate goal. And, hey, when you think about it, you actually enjoy the challenge of expanding a business, upping the ante, looking for the next big thing, and making a pile of money along the way. For you, there's nothing like the sheer joy of stomping on the gas and feeling your business lay a little rubber.

And when you *really* think about it, when you're really honest with yourself, most of you (including me) have to admit that you want to be big. You'd like to be out in front of the pack, with all the money, power, and recognition that goes with the lead. You itch to be rich and have the freedom to do what you want—and this small business isn't doing it for you.

If you were content, you wouldn't be reading this book. Like most business owners, you want to grow. How fortunate—because you're the person I wrote this book for.

As Big as You Like

Almost every business I come across has the potential for substantial growth; most of their operators just don't know how to get there. A few owners are most comfortable with an operation in which they know all their employees, the financial winds are light to moderate, and they can take the family on vacation for a few weeks and not worry about what Warren Buffett thinks. But the vast majority want to look in the mirror and see an Elephant.

What sort of elephant are you?

Well, yes, you think, of course I want my business to grow, but, come on, will I ever be Wal-Mart or Microsoft? Probably not, so why should I try to become the Elephant? The odds of that are about the same as my chances of opening a scuba shop on the moon.

You're forgetting that Elephants come in different sizes, but all Elephants have a few things in common: They're all companies big enough to make a difference, healthy enough to withstand strong financial winds, and strong enough to influence their market, whatever that market might be.

When you're an Elephant, you have power, wisdom, and respect.

Becoming an Elephant means growing your company to a size that's as big as *you* want. For some—me, for example—the goal is to be huge. For others, medium size is more comfortable; for still others, being a small Elephant is just fine.

Even if you genuinely wish to stay small, you need to become the Elephant in your neighborhood. If you don't, the fickle marketplace may assign that title to one of your competitors—and no one likes living under the feet of an Elephant.

In short, you can be an Elephant—and reap Elephant benefits—without being in the Fortune 500.

Whatever size Elephant you are, you will have built-in cash reserves and access to resources that, as a smaller company, you cannot expect to enjoy. You will have more employees, but they will make your life easier by providing you (and themselves) greater job security. You might have more day-to-day problems, but you'll have more people to handle them for you, more revenue to pay for processes and assistance. And if you hire wisely and organize well, you will have more days to spend sailing.

Why Did I Write This Book?

When I set out to put these ideas on paper, I had one goal in mind: to create the playbook that I wish I had had when I was building my businesses, a voice of experience to tell me what works and what doesn't in a no-BS style. Since those early years, I've had the advantage of spending a lot of time with successful business owners and applying my ideas successfully to scores of businesses, and I've found that the strategies and principles I discuss here work, not only in the United States, but everywhere.

Be the Elephant is the second book in a series aimed at helping solve the real issues faced by business owners, professionals, sales professionals, managers—anyone charged with growing any part of a business. The central idea of the first book, *Bag the Elephant,* was to provide a strategy for getting and keeping that huge customer. The book you're holding now focuses on a process and strategy you can implement to grow your business safely and efficiently—and become the Elephant yourself.

What Are You Worried About?

Growing a business is not easy. I should know—I've done it countless times. I've had some failures, but many successes to more than make up for them. Knowing when and how to grow effectively while keeping your eye on the current business is always a challenge.

You probably are asking yourself the same questions I've had to ask myself many, many times in the past:

- Should I be selling new things to the same customers? Or the same things to new customers?
- Should I be looking at a geographical expansion?
- When is the best time to expand?
- How can I make sure that my business is on solid footing and can handle the growth?
- How can I get a customer to fund my growth?
- How can I identify and mitigate the killer mistakes that can bury my company?

- What about risk?
- What about my employees? Will I alienate the others if I promote one or two to run the new venture?
- How will my current customers feel about my business expansion? Will they worry that I won't have time for them?
- What if it doesn't work? What then?

This book addresses all of these issues and more. I've spent the last five years designing and refining this strategy and have successfully applied it to the thirty-plus businesses I've owned or designed strategies for and the hundred-plus for which I've consulted in the United States, Europe, and Asia.

How to Use This Book

Read the whole thing. It's not that long. I've written it in clear, concise language. Don't just jump ahead to the growth strategy without reading and understanding the material on getting your business in shape; you need the whole package, starting with a solid foundation, in order to achieve lasting growth. If your business isn't on solid footing, then growth may simply bring about collapse.

Pass it on to everyone in your company charged with new-business development or growing even a piece of the business. Make sure all your salespeople read it so they can expand the business they do, and yours in the bargain. It's a great motivational tool, and it will help them reach their full potential.

Include your team. It's vital that your vision is shared with your whole team, whether you have one or one thousand employees. Nurturing the proper growth culture is paramount to success.

Be advised: I'm not promoting some get-rich-quick thing here. This is hard work. You'll have to buckle down and get ready to hear how it really is, in plain talk. Business clichés are a waste of time and I don't believe in varnishing the truth. I like to roll up my sleeves and dig in. If you're ready to do the same, then join me. If not, pass this book along to someone who can use it.

All My Children

The process of making a business successful has always fascinated me, and success, to me, means growth—big growth. I like to take small but promising businesses and turn them into big, healthy businesses. I like to create jobs, develop products, services, and people, and enhance commerce in its truest form. I marvel at how a capable businessperson can create solid value out of the thin air of ideas and ambitions. On the other hand, I'm also astounded at how seemingly smart people can work very hard on businesses that, because of a flawed business model, have no chance of success.

I've owned and run many businesses, and I've come to think of them as my children. Like an infant, a startup business is helpless, dependent entirely upon the parent. The child needs values, attention, love, and security. It needs someone to show it the way. Success means turning that infant into a healthy and productive adult that can stand on its own and command admiration and respect.

Between infancy and adulthood lies a vast field of challenges and options. As parents raising children and making crucial decisions, we often find our hearts leading one way and our minds another. Choose unwisely, and the process will fail, usually in a costly, painful way. Choose well, and you will be rewarded handsomely.

Wake up. Stand up. Look around you. See all the Elephants?

It's time to Be the Elephant.

Part I

BEGINNINGS

"Growth is not only desirable, but necessary.
To last, you have to grow."

The Hard Work
of Standing Still

D avenport Fine Furniture had been making and selling handcrafted furniture for fifty-three years. The owner, Barbara Davenport, inherited the company from the founder, her father. Annual sales were $1 million—not gangbusters, but still, not bad for a small, family-owned business.

Want to guess what a typical year's profits were? Ninety thousand.

That's pretty puny for a $1 million business, and Barbara's son Gene knew it. He joined the company two years ago to bring some new ideas and energy into the stagnant family enterprise.

Gene knew that, with such weak profitability, Davenport Fine Furniture was on the verge of collapse. The slightest shock—a sudden shortage of hardwood, a spike in transportation costs, the loss of a top salesperson—could mean the end for Davenport.

Gene, already a savvy businessman, applied some innovative thinking to the problem. He wanted to increase the number of distributors, upgrade to a semiautomated manufacturing process, and develop a midpriced product to better meet furniture-buying trends. He wanted the company to grow.

Before long, however, Gene ran into a brick wall—his mother. Barbara was reluctant to change. After all, she *was* getting by. Why rock the boat—or rocking chair, as it were? Of course, she was working herself into an early grave, but she wouldn't admit it.

Gene tried to persuade her that the bigger risk was in *not* growing. Not only were they vulnerable to the slightest glitch within the business, but the competition could overtake them at any time. Disaster could strike in any of a hundred ways. With such low profit margins and almost no cash reserves, the business would not be able to ride out even a modest downturn in sales. But everything he said just made Barbara more fearful—and stubborn.

> **It happens every day. Businesses that are not growing are dying, one by one.**

Gene stuck with it for a year. Finally, frustrated that none of his ideas were even seriously considered, let alone implemented, Gene left the business. Six months later, the business left the land of the living.

You can probably think of dozens of businesses where you used to shop that are no longer in existence. One day you're chatting about the weather with the guy behind the counter; next day, the front door is locked, the sign says CLOSED. The business that has served you for so many years is history.

It happens every day. Businesses large and small that are not growing are dying, one by one. Costs are rising; profits are shrinking. Technology is changing. Business is becoming global. Customers are driving out to the new big-box stores to buy their food, clothing, furniture, hardware, paint, and lumber. That small corner café that's been scraping by for twenty-five years? Watch what happens when a giant national coffee chain opens up stores on the other three corners. See the camera shop next door? It's getting steamrollered by technology that lets people take digital pictures and turn out crystal-clear prints instantly in their own home. Standing still, refusing to consider growing, is like setting up a lemonade stand in the middle of a busy highway: Now you see it, now you don't.

The Fear of Fear Itself

It's a sadly common story. Every year, thousands of Davenports bite the dust after scraping along for years at minimum profitability. Many owners in many industries think that, as long as they're paying their bills, everything is rosy. Their ambitions are modest; they like the idea of staying small, not making too much noise, not tempting the fates. But their decision to stay small isn't really a lifestyle choice—and it certainly isn't a sound business decision, either. It's a choice motivated by fear, which comes in several different flavors:

- Sometimes the fear masquerades as denial. Some business owners are selectively blind. They think that because the business is *their* business, their pride and joy, it is somehow exempt from the laws of both business and nature.
- Sometimes it is the fear of risk. They have a mortgage to pay off, some maxed-out credit cards, a kid or two in college. They're fighting to make ends meet, and any hiccup could be fatal. They feel stuck. And they're right—but it's this mindset that has allowed the business to become so fragile.
- Sometimes it's the fear of not knowing how to proceed. Growth is seen as a mysterious thing, fraught with obstacles and perils that smarter businesses know how to overcome.
- Sometimes it's the fear of admitting defeat. They're so invested in the status quo that changing or growing feels tantamount to defeat. Guess what? While these folks are afraid of admitting defeat, they're guaranteeing it.
- Sometimes it's the fear of the loss of tradition. They like their old business philosophy and don't want to change it. They feel that if they work really hard and give great service, the business will come—despite years of evidence to the contrary. As with Davenport Fine Furniture, the entrenched older generation won't let change happen.

Do you identify with any of these fears? My advice is always the same. If you're the owner and want your business to be a success, you've got to find the courage to change. Otherwise, you have to rely on luck to stay afloat, or hope for a miracle if you expect to grow. You still may be doing all right now because you know the business inside out, but what happens if you fall ill or decide to leave the business? This question is usually enough to start owners thinking about how close to the edge they are running, how little margin for error their business enjoys.

As for those who are working for companies on the Snail Trail, I advise them to take a careful look at their personal goals. If their long-term goals include financial success or career advancement, they should think about moving on— even if it's a family business, where familial loyalty must be weighed against career success.

The End . . . or the Beginning

I wrote this chapter with just one purpose in mind: to persuade you that growth is not only desirable, but necessary. To last, you have to grow. If you don't grow, then it's probably only a matter of time till your business bites the dust. You may point to successful small businesses here and there and tell me I'm mistaken, that I'm exaggerating, but the statistics are on my side. Big time.

So, if I've convinced you that you need to grow, that growing is a desirable thing to do, and you're ready to get going, read on.

Map It Out or Mess It Up

Fitness fanatic Thomas Leary owned Vitrex, a health products store in Phoenix. Tom's life mission was to convert complacent couch potatoes into muscular iron men like himself. He competed as a bodybuilder and spent most of his nonworking hours hiking and biking. Vitrex was his dream—a place where he could make the world healthier, one convert at a time.

Tom's customer base was local. He decided to expand beyond his one retail store by targeting customers who bought vitamins and other health-related products over the Internet. He set up his website, complete with an online point-of-sale program, e-commerce and fulfillment software, and a strong search-engine presence, and kicked it off with a massive online advertising campaign.

Sales quickly poured in. In just thirteen months, Vitrex's annual sales increased from $325,000 to $1.1 million. Business was great—so great that Tom caught growth fever. He expanded his product line, remodeled his brick-and-mortar retail space, and added staff to handle the new business. He had to work fifteen hours a day instead of ten, but he was living large and loving life.

Things seemed to go smoothly for another year. Then it happened.

It started with a few random calls from customers who were upset because they were being billed for orders they hadn't yet received. Then the volume of online orders caused outages and downtime on the website. Internet sales plummeted as online buyers grew wary and spread the word.

After four months of this, Vitrex had wasted away to a ninety-pound weakling. Even its core business had withered. So much of the company's energy and attention had been shifted to the new initiatives that longtime customers felt they were being neglected. Once the dust had settled on Vitrex's disastrous Internet effort, Tom turned his attention back to his original business and was surprised to see how many longtime members had cut their ties with Vitrex and gone to other health stores. He had grown, all right—smaller.

Proceed with Caution

Tom's story is a cautionary tale for anybody in business who wants to grow. The lesson? Growth *without planning* is risky business—often riskier than not growing at all.

The fact that you've read this far tells me that you want your company to grow. And there's no reason it shouldn't. But the story of Vitrex is all too common. Most companies that grow experience the same problems, and many of them fail when you would least expect them to fail: after a rapid increase in sales volume—either by gaining many new customers, as was the case with Vitrex, or from a single giant customer, as in the Elephant strategy I discussed in my previous book, *Bag the Elephant.*

How can these businesses experience disaster after a monumental increase in sales revenue? The most common reason is that they fail to plan for growth. In a nutshell, their infrastructure won't support a bigger business. Whether you entice one Elephant to buy your goods and services, or just a whole lot of ordinary customers, you're biting off a lot more than you can chew if you haven't done the planning necessary to handle the flow. You wouldn't throw a dinner party for twenty-four people with only five place settings. You wouldn't build an international air terminal with only five passenger gates. You wouldn't open a 500-seat restaurant with five waiters. Why would you promise customers 500 cakes a day out of a five-oven bakery?

It's not just a question of size, of course, but people too. Employees accustomed to doing business in a low-volume environment may not be ready to take on the newer, faster, more efficient methods required by a higher work flow. People in sales may not realize that the business cannot support the higher demand they are busy creating. Suppliers who were able to deliver raw materials for a smaller operation may be completely unable to meet the demands of your expanded business. Service personnel who deal with a few minor complaints from friendly, hometown customers may be hit with an avalanche of angry phone calls from strangers with a lot of money and market influence. If this unfolding disaster is not checked, the fast-growing business can spin out of control in a tornado of operational explosion, customer dissatisfaction, plummeting sales, and financial disaster. I call this kind of company the Shooting Star—and I think you can see why.

Harnessing the Energy

Fortunately, it's not always fatal. Some fast-growing but unprepared companies (the lucky ones), manage to keep the business going for a while by masking the problems or applying quick fixes on the fly. But quality usually suffers from either a lack of customer service in critical areas or an overall decline in quality. A common attitude among Shooting Star owners is, "Just sell the stuff, we'll figure out the operations later." Their growth is exclusively sales driven.

The sad thing about the Shooting Star is that in almost all cases the inevitable hit could have been avoided simply by knowing what to do. In Vitrex's case, Tom could have:

- created a more robust inventory supply and system, complete with backup suppliers,

- developed a customer service function to respond quickly to the issues, and
- anticipated the effects that the increase in volume might have on his website.

Well, he didn't think of these potential problems until it was too late—and, like many businesspeople who experience the heady rush of a booming business, he got a bit dazzled by the bucks as well.

To Be the Elephant

There are three essential factors for sustainable, successful growth:

- **Sales.** Growing by simply increasing sales rarely works in the long run—but sales provides the cash flow necessary to pay the bills. Cash flow is the lifeblood of the business; you simply cannot function without it. Sales revenue, once it has covered expenses, yields profit that can be used to compensate yourself and others and to reinvest in the business.
- **Infrastructure.** Without a solid organizational infrastructure, your business will quickly hit limits on customer service and production, miss growth opportunities, swallow up both your professional and personal life, even destroy itself. With the proper infrastructure, not only can the business handle growth, you'll be free to pursue your own destiny, whether it's running a larger business or exploring new horizons.
- **Knowledge.** Knowing what to do and having the courage to do it are two different things. I always had the courage, but when I started out I lacked the knowledge. I desperately needed someone to cut through the BS and tell me what was important and what wasn't, what to do and what to expect in return. I had to learn the hard way, by doing things wrong, but eventually I got it right.

In these pages, you'll also learn from the experiences of others. To protect both the guilty and the innocent, I've disguised the identities of the people and companies involved.

The secret to successful growth is to approach it as a solid, well-thought-out project, the same way you would approach starting a new business from scratch. Controlled, sustained, profitable growth is part art and part science. It helps to have a feel for the marketplace and the competition, but nothing can take the place of knowledge: knowing whether your current business is ready for growth; knowing which of several growth opportunities has the best chance of success; knowing how to capitalize on that opportunity while minimizing your risk.

Growing successfully takes ideas, effort, action, and commitment to long-term goals. It's a little like a buffet, in that you can select from a number of strategies and choose the best of many opportunities. But when you're through the line, it's best to end up with a complete, balanced meal on your plate. Otherwise, you may do yourself more harm than good.

Hungry? Let's dig in.

Part II
ON SOLID GROUND

"Many people say they have a sound business, and truly believe it, when in fact they have no idea whatsoever whether it's true."

Think You're Ready to Grow?

Be the Elephant focuses on strategies for growing your business effectively, but before you can even consider growing, you've got to make sure that the foundation of your current business is rock solid. You need to know that you're set up for success.

Some see business as the art of turning dreams into money, but the aspect of business I'm talking about—number crunching and analysis—is more about science, and it's essential. Without numbers, business is just expensive gambling, with your own and other people's money.

What's that? You're a swashbuckling entrepreneur, not an accountant? I disagree. I'd say that you're a gambler, not a businessperson.

Some might find it a bit boring. Maybe it is, but I say that growing and running a successful business is really a ton of fun. When you're successful, your investors, vendors, customers, and the people who work for you will have more fun, too. So, suck it up and get this done. The allure of risk? That's for the 70 percent who don't last three years, not me.

Many people say they have a sound business, and truly believe it, when in fact they have no idea whatsoever whether it's true. After you've finished part II, however, you'll know one way or the other. If your business is solid, you'll be ready to go to the next step—and grow! And if it's not, you'll have taken the first step toward fixing it.

Without numbers, business is just expensive gambling, with your own and other people's money.

What do we mean when we say "business model"? Quite simply, it's a set of schedules that demontrates specifically how your business is going to make money. It quantifies the assumptions you're making that lead to your profit projections. It weaves together your product, pricing, expenses, profits, risks, income sources, and cash-flow timing. It's a live document, a tool that you should use to shape your business for success.

Don't confuse business model with business plan. The business model tells you (and your investors) how your business will make its money, how much it will make, and when. The business plan is more comprehensive, and every business should have one. It includes detailed marketing strategies, sources of funding, corporate governance, and such. Business plan templates are widely available in books and online (see, among others, the federal government's Small Business Administration website at **www.sba.gov**).

Here we will focus on the business model, which I consider more practical and indicative of success. Unlike the business plan, which is mainly a start-up roadmap, the business model should be used continually to monitor and shape your business. You'll need a business model for each growth strategy you pursue, as well; it will tell you what works and what doesn't.

Business Is Great (I Think)

Of the 300,000-plus businesses that open every year in the United States, most are gone in less than three years. Why? Simply because many of them should never have been opened in the first place. They had no chance of success. If only the owners had run the numbers—done a business model—they would have seen it was flawed. They would have avoided all the headaches, stress, and disappointment of failure.

Why do so many business owners wait until it's too late to do a business model? Often it's a combination of eagerness and overconfidence: This is a great business idea! After all, it's *your* idea! How could it fail? You've done some math on the back of a napkin, and it works. It's all guesswork, anyway. Besides, you feel lucky.

Luck plays a part in success, but it shouldn't take the lead role. If you don't do the legwork necessary to make sure your business is meeting its expectations, failure is nearly inevitable. You might be making a profit, but are you selling enough to stay in business over the long run? Are your expenses going to become a problem? You may be getting by on cash flow, but what happens when you lose your biggest customer?

Unless you've just started, you've got some history in this business. That means you can use real figures in your business model, not just estimates. And when it comes to growth projections, you don't want to pile estimates on estimates; you need to know exactly how your business is performing now, and whether it can handle large increases in sales, production, and their associated expenses.

I once acquired a small marketing and promotion company that specialized in marketing to children. The company was losing about $100,000 per year. On the face of it, buying such a company sounds like a crazy move, but in truth it was the best purchase I ever made.

> **If you don't do the legwork necessary to make sure your business is meeting its expectations, failure is nearly inevitable.**

What drew me in? I worked up the business model for the company, using the same analytical tools I'm going to show you in the next few chapters. My analysis showed that although the company was headed for failure on its current path, changing a few critical components of the business model could turn the company into a big winner.

First, I charged higher fees to fewer clients, reduced costs like rent and back-office expenses, reduced risk exposure, streamlined operations, gave myself only a modest salary during the first few years, and hired sales professionals with more experience. By so doing, the company generated enough cash not only to support its growth, but also—just as important—to quickly pay off its debt.

The marketing company turned into a great business that I grew to love. I spent the next eight years working twelve hours a day, seven days a week, to drive its growth before selling it. I attribute that success to reshaping the business model early on.

> **The first thing you must understand: You have a huge bias toward believing your business will succeed.**

If you have not developed and analyzed a business model for your current business, I urge you to do so immediately. Most of the business decisions you make will be far more effective if they are based on a sound business model; without one, achieving success will be little more than a crapshoot. Before you even think about expanding your business, now's the time to see if it's on solid ground—and if it isn't, to *find* some solid ground.

Staying Real

When analyzing your current business model, the first thing you must understand is this: *You have a huge bias toward believing it will succeed.*

The reasons are obvious. You've no doubt dreamed of a big financial windfall and the prestige of being a winning entrepreneur, and you've already invested a lot of time, energy, and perhaps money in your idea.

Put away your rose-tinted glasses. Beware of common traps that tempt us all. When considering local competition, for example, we're inclined simply to think that we're different and better, or that our lower prices will steal everyone else's business. These are hunches at best; unless you've done your homework and can definitively say

Famous First (and Last) Words

Here are a few of the fatal hunches I've encountered over the years from overly optimistic business owners:

"People are dying for this stuff. We won't be able to meet the demand."

"I have a knack for this kind of thing. It runs in the family."

"Everybody loves pizza."

"All we have to do is make a few people aware of our product and we're home free."

"If my brother-in-law can make money with this in Cleveland, I'll make a mint with it here."

"Let's just figure the product will cost us $5 to make—after all, how much can it really cost?"

"Once I get the business going, I can make any adjustments it might need."

"My contacts from my last job will bring in enough business."

"I can sell anything to anyone."

"I'll get the sales now and figure out later how to deliver."

"This is my neighborhood. I know the people, and they know me."

"My partner's connections will make the business huge."

"By cutting back on service I can save a few bucks. Who's really going to notice?"

"Let's hire twenty more employees right now. I'm sure the revenue will come."

something like, "We spoke to 200 people in the area and 80 percent said they would switch to our business if we were better or cheaper," your theory is no more than speculation. Homework and research will turn your hunches into valid assumptions—or, more important, correct them and spare you a lot of grief.

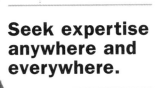

Seek expertise anywhere and everywhere.

Jenny Austin learned this lesson the hard way. She opened up a local coffeehouse— One Lump or Two—that sold premium and gourmet coffee for the price of regular coffee. The neighborhood already had several other coffee shops, as well as bookstores and restaurants where customers could grab a cup of joe. About six months after Jenny opened her store, I noticed a GOING OUT OF BUSINESS sign in the window. When I asked her what had happened, she seemed perplexed and told me how convinced she'd been that people would flock to her store for coffee. After all, her coffee tasted better and cost less.

Jenny had fallen into the hunch trap. She assumed that people would gravitate to her shop to save a few cents and savor a tastier brew. But people are creatures of habit and often choose their coffee provider for the ambience or convenience, not the price or quality. Her competitors all had customer loyalty on their side, not to mention the attractions of meals or books for customers who like to stretch out their coffee breaks. Had Jenny actually taken the time to test her hunch, she might have spared herself a great disappointment. She could have positioned her product differently, changed her product altogether, or even taken a pass on the entire venture.

The Five Keys to a Growth Mindset

Being objective and open to criticism about your business model can be difficult, especially once your business is up and running. Understanding my Five Keys to a Growth Mindset will help you keep a balanced perspective.

1. Acknowledge the downside. Understand how hard it is to create and own a successful business. Many businesses collapse within the first year or two. You've probably put up your own hard-earned money already, and so have family, friends, or other investors. Remember that people are investing in you as much as in your idea.

As you seek to understand your business's actual—rather than imagined—potential, keep in mind that you could lose everything you and others have put in. What would such a failure do to your finances? Your family? Your business? Imagining the worst-case scenario will inspire you to conduct your analysis more cautiously, and thereby greatly enhance your chances of success.

2. Consult with others. Evaluating your business should be a team effort. I've found that businesses whose owners are receptive to input have fared better than those whose owners try to do everything themselves. Seek expertise anywhere and everywhere. Network in your industry—you'll be surprised at how many people will be eager to help you. It flatters people to be consulted for their knowledge and skill, and most will oblige by sharing it.

3. Think numbers. This just may be the most important of the principles. Remember that you are trying to minimize guesswork. The best way to do that is to shoot for specifics. Don't rest until you can cite statistics or other hard numbers to support or refute your assumptions. If you believe, for example, that consumers will switch to your coffee shop because of better quality and lower prices, prove it. Interview a hundred customers from other coffee establishments and do the math. I'll show you how in the next chapter.

4. Invite criticism. Every business analysis needs a devil's advocate—someone who doubts everything, pokes holes everywhere, and comes up with so many pitfalls and what-ifs that you are ready to scream. Better to scream now than when facing bankruptcy because you didn't foresee the dangers.

Kaplan's Five Keys to a Growth Mindset

1. Acknowledge the downside.

2. Consult with others.

3. Think numbers.

4. Invite criticism.

5. Temper your enthusiasm with reason.

> **Enthusiasm is a 500-horsepower engine, and you need a sober and vigilant driver behind the wheel.**

Surround yourself with people who will tell you what they really think, not just what they think you want to hear. It defies human nature to tell friends things you know may upset or disappoint them (a challenge I face routinely when people ask me to review their business ideas). Reassure them that you will not be offended by their reactions, however harsh, and that spotting potential downsides is the best way they can help you. Don't undermine the criticism process by politely listening, then simply dismissing all input that doesn't agree with your preconceptions and hopes. Remember, you *want* to know the potential problems so you can avoid them or solve them in advance.

5. Temper your enthusiasm with reason. Strive to be pragmatic, even stoic, when evaluating your business. Resist the urge to delude yourself with sunny projections. Even if the business looks bulletproof on the surface, you need to probe it for inner weaknesses. Enthusiasm is a 500-horsepower engine, and you need a sober and vigilant driver behind the wheel.

The Guts
of the Model

W hat are assumptions? In plain English, they're simply the numbers—and the rationale behind them—that you plug into your business model to find the answer to the question of whether your business will survive, thrive, or die. These numbers are not guesses that you pull out of thin air; they are refined estimates based on thorough research and verifiable fact. Nothing less can serve as the basis for the momentous decisions you must make to ensure success in business. We will talk about two kinds of assumptions: revenue assumptions and cost assumptions.

For effective business modeling and decision making, you'll need to plug these assumptions into several schedules—data tables—that are the components of a standard business model. If you're not careful, you can overload and go a bit crazy with information. The trick is to sift through the maze of data and focus only on what you need. That's what we're going to do here. (Don't sweat it; it's easier than you might think.)

This section will tell you precisely what information and assumptions you will need to make sure your business is in good health and ready to grow. Once we nail the assumptions, we can focus on the four schedules most essential for evaluating both a current and a new business.

To simplify the concepts I'll use an actual example, Argosy Audio and Video, and walk you through the process of generating assumptions. Argosy sells home theater systems and audiovisual components to consumers and businesses. Argosy also has a service department that travels to homes and businesses. The company makes money as well by promoting warranties for its products and offering subscribers programming options such as DirecTV.

Revenue Assumptions

You use revenue assumptions to develop your overall sales projections. They reflect how much money you expect the business to bring in for the foreseeable future. To produce a reliable figure, you'll need to understand the various ways your business makes money; how many potential customers you will have in a day, week, or month; how many of these potential customers will end up making a purchase; how much you'll charge for your product or service; and the number of business days you plan on being open. I recommend the following three steps:

Fit Assumptions to Your Business

If you're not in retail but in another type of business, such as a B2B operation, you may need to define projected sales by product line, salesperson, or account over a specified period such as a season, a quarter, or your own selling cycle.

Step 1: List all revenue streams.

Revenue streams are the ways your business makes money. (As you will learn in part IV, chapter 11, revenue streams are made up of all the sources of revenue your business draws upon, but for our purposes here, we can lump these into several distinct categories of similar products or services that we call revenue streams.) List all of these streams of revenue, including the less obvious ones, like Argosy's warranty business, or rental income if you own your building and lease out space to another business.

Include revenue streams that you're committed to adding to the business, such as new products, new services, or new ways of selling your products or services to other businesses or markets.

Argosy, for example, has five revenue streams:
- In-store items (home theaters and components for individuals)
- Commercial products (systems for small businesses)
- Home servicing (installation, maintenance, and repairs)
- Warranty sales (extended warranties)
- Programming commissions (DirecTV and other subscriber services)

Step 2: For each revenue stream, record the following.

Overview. Briefly outline how each revenue stream brings in money. Be as detailed as you can for each product and service. Argosy's in-store item stream, for example, consists of both home theater systems and their components. Both make money in sales to customers at the retail store. The warranty business earns money by selling extended warranties to customers who have purchased components; the commercial products target small-business owners; programming sales come from customers who have purchased televisions and home theaters.

Sales plan. Indicate how you plan to sell the products and services you listed above. Answer in detail, even if you plan to rely on brokers, referrals, or government contracts to generate sales. If you intend to hire salespeople, how many? Will they share responsibilities? At Argosy, for example, the same people sell components and home theaters. Make sure to allocate accurately the time spent selling each product line—for example, Argosy's salespeople spend one third of their time on theaters and two thirds on components. Of course, many companies, especially at start-up, will have one salesperson—you. Nevertheless, you still need to jot down your sales plan.

Revenue Assumption Worksheet: Argosy Audio and Video

The information on this worksheet summarizes detailed workup sheets for each assumption:

General Revenue Stream	Stream Overview	Sales Plan	Number of Salespersons	Potential Customers per Day	Conversion to Sale	Units Sold per Day	Average Price	Business Days per Year	Annual Revenue
In-store items	Selling home theaters	Sales force, in-store	2	30	4%	1.2	$4,500	270	$1,458,000
	Selling components	Sales force, in-store	4	15	20%	3.0	$340	270	$275,400
Commercial products	Selling to businesses	Sales force, field and phone	2	30 calls out	2%	0.6	$4,800	220	$633,600
Home servicing	Labor & parts	Inbound phones, customer service	1	9	90%	8.1	$46	230	$85,698
Warranty sales	Selling extended warranties	Sell with existing products at checkout	All (8)	3	30%	0.9	$12	270	$2,916
Programming sales	Commissions from selling programming products such as DirecTV	Included as part of overall sale	All (8)	20	10%	2.0	$14	270	$7,560

Potential customers. Include the number of prospects your salespeople will interact with each day, including phone contacts (it might be more practical to do this on a weekly rather than a daily basis). You might also find it helpful to classify them according to customer types appropriate to your business and industry—for example, business, residential, walk-in versus appointment, local versus regional.

Conversion to sale. What percentage of your prospects will buy? Conversion-to-sale figures vary widely among industries and even within one company at different times. At first you might use an industry average as your estimate, but as your business grows, it will become more and more important to monitor conversions to sale for each of your salespeople and revenue streams, not only for the data but because raising this conversion ratio is one of the most effective ways to boost profits.

Units sold. Record how many units each salesperson will sell each day. How many does that amount to per week, per month, and per year? Perform this exercise for each product or service.

Average price. Record the price you will charge for each unit or service. Then calculate how much the average customer sale will be. Be sure to consult comparable businesses as well as industry publications and trade associations.

Business days per year. Estimate how many days you will be open each year. The number may vary among your different revenue streams. Argosy's commercial products business, for example, closes for the weekend while its retail outlets stay open Saturday.

Step 3: Project total company revenue.

For each revenue stream, perform the following three calculations.

1. Calculate the number of units sold each day by multiplying the number of potential customers per day by the conversion-to-sale ratio for that unit. Here's an example:

Revenue Stream	Prospects	×	Conversion	=	Units/Day
In-store home theater	30		4%		1.2
In-store components	15		20%		3.0
Commercial	30		2%		0.6
Home servicing	9		90%		8.1
Warranty	3		30%		0.9
Programming	20		10%		2.0

2. Calculate the total annual revenue for each stream by multiplying the number of units sold each day by the average price per unit, then multiplying the result by the number of business days the unit will be available each year.

Revenue Stream	Units/ Day	×	Average Price/Unit	×	Business Days/Year	=	Total Annual Revenue
In-store home theater	1.2		$4,500		270		$1,458,000
In-store components	3.0		$340		270		$275,400
Commercial	0.6		$4,800		220		$633,600
Home servicing	8.1		$46		230		$85,698
Warranty	0.9		$12		270		$2,916
Programming	2.0		$14		270		$7,560

3. Calculate the total company revenue. After you find the annual total for each revenue stream, simply add the sums together to determine the total annual revenue for your business. The total annual company revenue assumption for Argosy is $2,463,174.

This snapshot of income assumptions is much more than a fancy way of arriving at a projected annual income. For example, it tells you that a slight conversion increase in selling home theaters would dwarf the rewards of a massive effort to triple warranty sales.

Strive to make each assumption as accurate as possible; even minor errors can turn your projected revenues on their head. For example, if Argosy converted only 1 percent of potential commercial customers into sales rather than 2 percent, it would sell $316,800 less than initially projected—enough to risk crippling the business.

Conversely, if the actual conversion ratio were 3 percent rather than 2 percent, the company's commercial business would have seen sales of $950,400—$316,800 more than assumed. That's a more desirable problem than a shortfall, of course, but ideally you'd want to be able to plan ahead for the windfall—perhaps to expand your business, acquire another business, or even take a vacation.

Cost Assumptions

Now that you've made your revenue assumptions, it's time to shift to costs. Cost assumptions are as important as revenue assumptions—it's just as perilous to underestimate costs as it is to overestimate revenues.

To organize your thinking about cost assumptions, it's a good idea to break costs into two categories: *operating expenses,* which you incur through the day-to-day running of your company, including rent, payroll, supplies, and taxes; and *cost of goods sold,* the costs you incur getting your products or services to market. This tends to be more of a typical accounting exercise, but it's a must.

Cost assumptions can be easier to calculate than revenue assumptions because you can get precise quotes for many expenses, you can control your hiring, and, depending on how long your company has been operating, you may have actual costs at your fingertips. The hardest part is not forgetting any of the many costs that your business might incur. Let's take a look at each of the cost categories.

> **Cost assumptions are as important as revenue assumptions—it's just as perilous to underestimate costs as it is to overestimate revenues.**

Operating expenses are your day-to-day business costs. They include both *fixed expenses* such as rent, utilities,

Operating Expenses

Fixed Expenses
Rent
Real estate taxes and CAM
　(common area maintenance)
Insurance
Other taxes

Variable Expenses
Payroll, including bonuses and
　commissions
Payroll taxes
Repairs and maintenance
Supplies
Utilities
Telephone
Professional services
Advertising
Travel and entertainment

Other Expenses
Loan payments—
　principal and interest

interest on debt, and insurance, and *variable expenses* such as payroll, payroll taxes, repairs, maintenance, utilities, advertising, and professional services from accountants, lawyers, or consultants. In determining operating expenses, keep your revenue assumptions handy—you'll need to account for all the costs you'll face in bringing in revenue.

Tackle the cost categories one by one. Add any other cost categories you can think of that apply to your business. This is one of the areas where it can pay to get expert help: If you have an operating business, have your accountant run an itemized income statement for you.

The cost of goods sold is what you spend getting your product to market. If you own a stationery store, for instance, your cost of goods sold would include your inventory—greeting cards, paper goods, specialty items—as well as the carrying bags for customers' merchandise and the tape, bows, ribbon, and wrapping paper used to wrap the gifts. If you're manufacturing a product, you'd include everything from the cost of the raw materials to packaging, even the costs of actually delivering the product to the store or other business for sale. Take particular care to include all relevant costs. If you have an established company, be sure to use your actual costs.

This is also a good time to reevaluate your costs of goods sold. Ask your current and potential suppliers to provide a price quote for each element of your cost of goods sold. Then you can compare quotes and either renegotiate prices or switch suppliers to reduce costs.

Harvesting Data

When it comes to gathering the necessary facts, there's no book to turn to, no magic formula to use, no mysterious service to retain. That said, you have many valuable methods at your disposal—and the more creative you are at finding them, the better. The important thing is to leave no stone unturned in unearthing the information you need, rather than giving up and just guessing.

Your best and most accurate information will come from your existing business, so use it whenever possible. If such data aren't available, consider the following resources, all of which I've found useful.

Competition. Fish around at a competitor—if not locally then in a similar town. Drop by to see how many people visit the business in a day, at peak hours, and on weekends. What do customers buy? How much do they buy at one time? Without being overbearing, talk to the customers yourself to get their take. Perhaps you'll learn that the business runs only a skeleton crew during slow periods, a strategy that might reduce your own payroll costs. Gather any information you can, including brochures, pricing sheets, menus, and promotional materials. Talk to the manager as well. As long as you remain pleasant, you'll be amazed at how many people will enjoy helping you.

I once had a friend named Steve who was starting a business that sold photocopiers. He took the trouble to learn the name of a competitor's top salesman, then got up at 6:00 A.M. every day for a week to follow the guy around. He counted the

Tips on Working with Assumptions

1. Keep track of how you arrive at each assumption. Even if you eventually decide to change methods, it's important to keep track of them, because you'll be reassessing your assumptions each time you review your business.

2. Ask people you respect to sound off on your assumptions.

3. Hedge your assumptions. Lower your revenues and increase your costs, each by 10 percent, a tactic that will protect you if something goes awry or your estimates prove too rosy.

4. Use appropriate time frames for your assumptions, whether daily, weekly, or monthly.

number and duration of sales calls and how often he performed a copier demo, the final step in selling a machine. I thought this was creative, effective, and, yes, bordering on excessive, but Steve respected the salesperson's privacy and kept his distance.

Consultants and experts. Some businesses retain industry consultants to help set up their operations. Make sure to check references before retaining any consultant, as you will want someone attuned to your specific needs and not interested solely in generating billable hours.

When I was asked to invest in a Minneapolis entertainment center (a story I tell in more detail in the next chapter), I contacted entertainment centers in other cities and spoke with several industry associations until I found the name of a consultant who had more than thirty years' experience in the industry. He charged me $300 for a two-hour consultation, during which he told me almost everything I needed to know about the industry based on his vast experience and success. Here are a few of the things I learned:

- The average annual revenue for a new bowling facility assumed 12,000 games per lane at $6 per game, a figure that included other sources of revenue such as bowling shoe rentals, pro shop sales, lounge and snack bar sales, and sales from a ten-game arcade. This gave me the basis for determining revenue assumptions for bowling in the Minneapolis facility:

$$12,000 \text{ (games/year/lane)} \times 25 \text{ (lanes)} \times \$6 \text{ (per game)}$$
$$= \$1,800,000$$

  To that figure I added sales figures from our other revenue streams, such as entrance fees to the water park. These projections were based on estimates that the consultant also shared with us. The total facility revenue was projected to be $3,100,000 per year.
- To succeed, a new facility should operate at 32 percent pretax margin (the percentage by which revenue exceeds expenses before income tax, depreciation, and amortization).

- Payroll should be no more than 20 percent of sales.
- Occupancy costs (rent, real estate taxes, and utilities) should be no more than 10 percent of sales.

Suppliers. Suppliers can be another great resource, though you should be wary of what they say, since they have a vested interest. Many salespeople for large companies have access to demographics and other useful industry information. I used to get market analysis and industry reports from the salesperson who handled our printing. Because he called on most of my potential customers, he had a wealth of information on industry spending patterns, including which companies were increasing their spending. Suppliers might also give you the scoop on your competitors, such as how much they are paying for services and other insider gossip.

Industry associations. Don't forget trade associations, particularly for information on recent trends. Many industry associations publish reports on salaries, revenue trends, and company rankings based on revenue, profitability, and more. If you cannot afford to join the association, you can still talk with an official, especially if you express interest in joining someday. More likely than not, a representative will send you a few reports or let you try out the association's resource service.

Explore every possible avenue when gathering information.

Trade magazines. Check out relevant trade publications. Many have resource guides, advertisements, and articles that may buttress your analysis. Look at the return information cards in the magazines and check the services that interest you. You can use this method to solicit information from your competitors or from other companies in the industry.

Conventions. Show up at conventions, local and out of town, and work the room. Talk to other attendees, vendors, and presenters. I've spoken at many such shows and am always thrilled to chat with people who approach me with questions so they might better understand their businesses.

Before the convention begins, make sure to get a program that lists speakers and exhibitors. Highlight which people you want to talk to. That way you'll have a better chance at meeting your networking goals. Consider contacting a speaker ahead of time to schedule a few one-on-one minutes. Don't be afraid to ask questions during the Q&A session.

Internet. With a click of the mouse, you can find nearly anything on the web these days, from a public company's earnings to a private company's business descriptions to pricing schedules and office locations. Plug key industry words into a search engine, then browse away. Visit your competitors' websites; you'll be surprised at how much you can learn.

Library. Take a trip to the library reference desk and ask for help in finding current information about your industry.

To maximize your information harvest, learn your industry's SIC (Standard Industrial Classification) code number, which you can find at your local public library's business section in the *Standard Industrial Classification Manual.* Use this number to sift through resources such as the *Annual Statement Studies,* also available at the library. This publication, put out by Risk Management Association, provides invaluable information broken out by company revenue size. Here you will find industry benchmarks for everything from cash and receivables percentages to gross profits, operating expenses, and more.

Other resources include the *Dun & Bradstreet Industry Handbook* and your library's computer banks. Sort by industry or SIC, then wade through the overviews, articles, profiles, and more. You can also seek information by looking up a comparable business and then extrapolating information for your own needs.

Interviews. Whenever you're hiring, pay close attention to applicants who are experienced in your industry. Sales, operations, and accounting people all have something to add to your store of information. By asking the right people the right questions, you can learn much about sales levels, pricing, the number of orders written each day, business margins, and more.

Four Statements
to Live By

ow it's time to crunch some numbers. Let me start by saying that I've never been particularly fond of numbers. As a matter of fact, I'd feel no sense of loss if I never saw another financial statement again in my life. I spent years running a big company with twenty-one offices in more than fifteen countries. During that time I saw many financial schedules and statements and came to the conclusion that many of them are overkill—not really needed.

However, you cannot expect to have a successful business if you don't do the numbers. You don't need to be a math whiz or a CPA, but you do need to have a good enough grasp of the numbers to know how much money you're going to bring in, to make sound business decisions, and to ensure that you can meet your payroll and pay bills. The one constant is that numbers don't lie—*if your assumptions are correct and you know what to look for.* Here's a good example of how understanding the numbers kept me from making a big mistake.

Water Under the Bridge

A few months ago I reviewed a business opportunity that came to me from a friend who wanted me to join him and his partners in what he called a "sure-fire" business venture. They had just opened Great Waves Fun Center, a 200,000-square-foot indoor water park and entertainment facility near Minneapolis. At first glance, the business sounded like a great idea: a huge water park with a lazy river and slides, hundreds of video and arcade games, bumper cars, bowling lanes, volleyball courts, a snack bar and grill, and a banquet facility to boot.

The Minneapolis location, with its many young families and teens, seemed ideal. The area was free of competitors, and Minnesota's severe winter weather, which forces people indoors, would help generate a lot of business. Even better, the community supported the project with gusto, and my potential partners boasted much talent and experience.

In other words, a slam dunk.

Not so fast. After I asked to see the business projections, I was surprised to discover that none existed. They had made a few fuzzy assumptions and some general cost estimates, and the senior partner had a vague idea of what future sales might be, but that was it. In all, the project required the partners to put up more than $3 million in start-up capital and sign a loan for another $1.5 million—yet everyone was operating in the dark.

> Owners who "have it all up here" rarely have the capability to build organizations.

When I met with the lead partner to express my concern about the lack of planning, he smiled and tapped his forehead. "It's all in here," he said. Now, *that's* a red flag if there ever was one. Owners who "have it all up here" rarely have the capability to build organizations. They don't like to delegate responsibility and don't respect the numbers—two huge issues that should make you very nervous.

He went on to boast that after only eight weeks the business was generating sales of more than $350,000 a month. I asked him how he knew that $350,000 a month was good. He looked at me as though I were crazy and asked what

I meant. I said that $350,000 sounded great, but what if the cost of operating the business each month was more than $350,000? Which he couldn't know, since the business was new and he had no projections.

Sadly, this sort of pie-in-the-sky approach is all too common among entrepreneurs, many of whom specialize in being in constant motion. They run in every direction and leave no time for planning, the most important activity of all.

I told the group that before deciding whether I would be interested in joining them, I needed to feel comfortable that the business had potential for success, based on solid business projections. The partners were justifiably concerned and agreed to work with me to develop a business model. After all, they had just made a decision that could change their lives forever; in addition to investing millions of dollars and mortgaging their homes, they would be devoting many hours to the business.

After spending some time with the lead partner trying to extract the various assumptions and information from his head and his notes, then meeting with a low-cost expert in the industry, what I learned was sobering:

- The cost of operating the business each month was, in fact, a little more than the $350,000 in sales. Because they had no large cash reserve, during the first year each of the partners would have to put even more money into the business just to pay the bills. And since it had already operated at a negative cash flow for two months, it would need to make up for the two months' shortfall, even if the business were adjusted. Hardly a solid foundation for growth!
- Under the current price and cost assumptions, it would take the business eight years to break even, and the partners wouldn't make any real profit for nearly a decade.
- The business's pretax earnings were only 8 percent of its sales, significantly less than the industry standard of 20 percent. That's a frightening sign that something is wrong.

- The rent, taxes, common area maintenance (CAM), and utilities for the facility were 35 percent of their projected sales—again, worse than the industry average of 28 percent—a sign that profits could be eternally weak.

These findings and others led to the same conclusion: The foundation of the company was very weak. In its current form, what seemed like a great opportunity was at best a long shot. At worst, the water park would turn into a financial bath.

What would have happened to the company in the absence of a financial analysis? Each month for at least the first year, they would have been forced to scrape around for more cash to run their business. For a decade or so, they'd work night and day to keep the company afloat, making little or no money in return—unless they went out of business first.

I presented my findings. After the shock passed, we had several more discussions and began to tear through the various schedules to shape the business into a profitable entity. With much hard work and many business adjustments—such as reducing payroll and retooling the pricing strategy—the business model looked much more encouraging. In fact, the partners could now expect to begin making a profit after three years. More important, the excess cash flow generated each month was enough to fund business operations without a further infusion of cash.

Keep yourself on schedule if you want to reach a profitable destination.

I passed on this opportunity, but recently I heard from my friend that the business was right on track. The revised business model was proving out.

The Four Horsemen of the Accountant

How did I know that the business, as originally set up, was destined for failure? The answer: a quick run through the schedules. I've boiled them down to a mere four that I consider essential for success in business:

1. Projected revenue statement
2. Projected cash flow statement
3. Projected income (profit/loss) statement
4. Projected balance sheet

You've got to develop these schedules in order to know whether your business is on the road to success. Ideally, you should do this before opening, but if you're already operating and haven't done so, you'd better get going—you might be on borrowed time.

But not to worry, because to spare you the agonizing flashbacks to Miss Wehrmachts's remedial math class, I'm not going to show you the walls of numbers involved in these schedules. However, I will talk about them in general terms in this chapter. If you wish to see the actual figures I used to analyze Great Waves, go online to **www.differencemaker.com** and click on "Freebies," where you will find all four schedules.

Whether you run a small business from your home or a large company with several offices and hundreds of employees, you should develop the same four schedules. The only difference might be the number of 000's on the statements.

If you are not a trained accountant, you shouldn't even think of putting these financial schedules together yourself. Many accountants have electronic templates in Excel or other common software, which allows them to work with you at low cost to develop the schedules for your business. You simply drop in the numbers (assumptions) for your projections. Make sure the worksheets are linked, so you can see the immediate effects when you adjust your assumptions—revenue and expenses—to find a business model that works.

Adjusting, Not Fudging

Throughout this chapter, I will be talking about revising your assumptions to shape a stronger business model. It's very important to understand that revising your assumptions does not mean fiddling with the numbers until the projections look good.

There are two valid ways to revise assumptions. The first involves getting better data. For example, after a business has been operating for a few months, you can replace estimated income, expenses, and other estimates with actual numbers. Or you can do more research and bring your estimates in line with industry averages. Using more accurate numbers can make your projections look better—or worse.

> **Revising your assumptions does not mean fiddling with the numbers until the projections look good.**

The second valid way of revising assumptions involves changing the way you plan to run your business. If you find that increasing the number of customers by 5 percent will increase projected profitability by 15 percent, it's not enough simply to revise that number upward; you must also figure out how to get those extra customers. If your expense assumptions make your cash flow look dangerous, and the main problem is your rent, you can't simply lower your rent estimate and think you've solved the problem; you also need to figure out how to run your business from smaller, less expensive premises.

Let's now have a look at these statements, one by one, to find out what they are and how they can help you.

Projected Revenue Statement

The projected revenue statement sorts your company's total projected revenues into separate revenue streams, each on its own line, month by month, using either a straight-line approach (annual revenue for the stream divided by twelve months) or seasonally, taking your business's peaks and valleys into account. You can display some revenue streams straight-lined and others seasonal as appropriate.

The revenue statement tells you the following:

- the various ways the company generates its revenue (revenue streams),
- the amount of revenue the company generates monthly and yearly for each stream, and

- the percentage of the total revenue represented by each revenue stream.

Each revenue stream is totaled. The grand total of all the individual revenue streams from this schedule is used as the revenue figure in the income (profit & loss) and cash flow statements. As such, revisions to the revenue statement will directly affect these other schedules.

Here's how to use the revenue statement to review and shape your business:

Revenue composition. Review each revenue stream and each revenue source within the stream to ensure that it should be a part of your business. Is it contributing enough to the overall revenue? Is it contributing so much of the total business that you're too dependent on it? Look at both the total dollar figure and the percentage of total revenue contributed by each stream.

Revenue opportunities. Analyze each revenue stream. Is there anything you can do to boost revenues in any or all of them? Can you get more from your salespeople? As realistically as possible, calculate the revenue growth each stream will achieve during the next five years. You need this figure to complete the projected income and cash flow statements.

Project these assumptions over the next five years. This will be your revenue growth plan and will provide numbers used in the future cash flow and income statements.

Projected Cash Flow Statement

The cash flow projection not only shows you how much cash your business will generate month by month—enabling you to pay your bills, run the company, and take money at the end of the year—but it also gives you a snapshot of your business's operating budget and tells you whether and when your business will start turning a profit.

You should expect to spend more time analyzing the projected cash flow statement than any other report. It can be a wonderful confidence builder, because it gives you a good idea of what's down the road. Ignore it, and you might spend endless, anxious hours working on your business, without knowing if you even have a chance of meeting your goals.

If your business is new or you haven't generated a cash flow statement, ask your accountant to project your cash flow on a

You should expect to spend more time analyzing the projected cash flow statement than any other report.

monthly basis for the first twenty-four months, then annually for years three through five. This is critical. If you still have projected debt after year five, extend the annual cash flow until two years after your debt is gone. Remember to include in your assumptions all start-up costs you'll incur before you even open or expand your business. If you never become profitable or aren't happy with the time to profitability, your decision is tough but simple: shape the assumptions to move up the date of profitability, or close up shop and move on.

Another crucial point to consider: If your business relies on credit cards or receivables, account for a percentage of noncollectible receivables. Uncollected bills have an impact on your cash flow. Noncollectible accounts receivable typically range from 2 to 5 percent of sales. Check your industry to be sure.

The cash flow statement tells you:

- whether you will have enough cash to pay your bills each month,
- your business's various operating expenses month by month,
- the month your business will have positive cash flow, taking into account all activities since its inception,
- the amount of cash available at the end of the year to reinvest or take as additional compensation,
- your monthly operating budget, and
- your cumulative cash flow into the future.

Here are the figures on the cash flow statement that are particularly important for both future and established businesses:

Monthly cash flow. Net cash flow is the amount of cash available each month after your monthly bills have been paid. Strive to have the business start making money consistently no later than month six. The time frame will vary depending on the potential of the business and the risk you are comfortable assuming. Remember, the monthly cash flow doesn't account for bills owed from prior months.

Cumulative cash flow. This is the total cash flow for the business since its inception. The figure includes all expenses incurred to date and is presented on a monthly basis to summarize the current cash situation.

Move through the months along the cumulative line until you reach the largest negative number. This represents your largest cash shortfall. Make sure your business can support every negative cash flow month—in other words, that its cash reserve exceeds this largest negative number.

If you're considering a new business or analyzing your current one, make sure you have access to enough cash to pay your bills for about a year and a half. If you can't get the business to throw off enough cash to pay the bills by then, or can't or don't wish to invest any more money to pay bills, don't open the business, or close it if it's open. Again, tough but simple.

Cash available for reinvestment or distribution at the end of the year. Assuming your business runs according to plan, how much cash will be available at the end of the year to reinvest, take as income, or pay off loans? To get this answer, begin with the total cash available at the end of the year and subtract enough money to begin the next year.

> **Strive to have the business start making money consistently no later than month six.**

Monthly operating budget. The expenses listed on the cash flow statement (cost of goods sold and operating expenses) can act, in effect, as a budget. Why? Because in order to achieve your cash flow expectations, not only must you meet your revenue projections, you also need to keep your expenses within expectations. Therefore, manage all line items and costs on the statement as a firm budget.

Under the operating expenses portion of the statement, you will see a breakout according to expense classification. Expenses are shown on a monthly basis for the first year, then as totals for future years.

Projected Income (Profit/Loss) Statement

The projected income statement shows revenues, gross profits, operating expenses, EBITDA (accounting shorthand for earnings or profits before interest expense, taxes, depreciation, and amortization), and net income on one schedule. This allows you to analyze your business performance on a yearly basis and compare it to future or past years.

Ask your accountant to put the projected income statements for a five-year period on a single statement. Along with total dollars, include the percentage of total revenue each expense represents. This makes it easy to measure your expenses against past and future performance as well as against industry standards.

The projected income statement tells you:

- company growth year-over-year: revenue, cost, EBITDA, and net income;
- comparative revenues and operating costs from year to year, and
- overall business success over an extended period.

Here's how the projected income statement helps you manage your business:

Company growth year-over-year. Compare results of operations from year to year by gauging growth or decline in revenue, gross profit percentage, EBITDA, and net income. Start by looking at each of these figures. The total sales should increase and expenses as a percentage of sales should decrease through the years. Analyze the figures carefully to make sure they're in line with your expectations.

EBITDA is the truest gauge of your business's operating performance. It is essentially net income without the impact of specific accounting activities that tend to muddy the picture, such as income tax, depreciation, amortization, and interest expense. For this very reason, many acquisition valuations are based on EBITDA. As you become more efficient, EBITDA should increase through the years in both total dollars and percent of gross revenue.

EBITDA is the truest gauge of your business's operating performance.

Efficiency of your operating business. Comb line by line through the expense and cost-of-goods-sold portions of your income statement to find areas of inefficiency. Use the percentage of sales to compare each of your expense items with comparable figures for your competitors, your previous year's performance, and industry averages. Although the total cost for each expense will probably increase as you grow, its percentage against total revenue should decline. Seek to make changes that lower your costs and thus boost your profits. The total dollars column will guide you to areas where you can make the biggest impact.

Projected Balance Sheet

The balance sheet provides a snapshot of a business's financial condition at a given time, usually the end of a fiscal year.

This is what the balance sheet tells you:

- how much cash the business will have at the end of the year,
- how much short-term and long-term debt the business will have, and
- the business's ability to pay its debts.

Here's how to use the balance sheet to answer the following questions:

How much cash is in the business? This figure is listed under the Current Assets heading as cash. Capital reserves, the money you might leave in reserve for emergencies, should also be included in this figure.

How much debt will the business have? The projected balance sheet reflects two kinds of debt based on when the debt is due: current, or short-term (up to twelve months), and long-term debt or liabilities (longer than twelve months).

Can your business pay its debts? I'm not big on formulas. However, I do rely on the current ratio formula, because it expresses a company's ability to pay its bills. You can calculate this ratio from the balance sheet by dividing your projected current assets by the projected current liabilities. Current ratio standards vary among industries, but, as a rule, strive to keep your current assets 50 percent larger than your current liabilities. This would leave you with a current ratio of 1.5:1.

6

What's the Downside?

You've put your assumptions on paper. You've developed the four schedules that tell you whether your business is on a sound footing and ready to handle growth. Now there's one more factor to consider: risk. How does risk affect your assumptions and your overall business model? How can you protect against the most dangerous risks—the ones that could kill your business?

Unless you're a glutton for emotional punishment, you won't find this part of the process especially pleasant. The forces that are beyond your control are the most worrisome, and there's no end to the risks a business might face. Could you lose your entire investment? Yes. Could a large competitor shove you aside and take over your market? Yes. Could a hurricane down on the coast 500 miles away affect your business? Maybe so; you'd better be prepared. Assessing risk is not fun, and it's not easy, but you have to plan for contingencies—especially if your risk analysis indicates that you should walk away from the business idea altogether.

Here are the steps you should take to assess the potential risks to your business:

1. Identify every possible risk you can think of, no matter how remote it may seem.

2. Assess how much control you have over each risk.

3. Rate both the likelihood that you'll encounter each risk and the severity of the consequences that will arise if you do.

4. Review the list to consider ways of mitigating each risk should it become a reality.

> **Assessing risk is not fun, and it's not easy, but you have to plan for contingencies.**

Let's walk through this process step-by-step. To begin analyzing them, group risks into three basic categories: business risks, personal risks, and external risks. The risk-assessment matrix near the end of this chapter will help simplify things for you.

Business Risks

These risks affect your business directly—your finances, operations, organization, or competitive position.

Financial risks. Many potential financial risks became apparent when you developed your revenue and cost assumptions. Consider those risks as well as the following:

- **Missed sales targets.** What happens to your business model if sales fail to meet expectations? Can you reduce expenses to make up the difference in profit?
- **Late payments.** What if your accounts pay late? Will you have enough cash to operate the business?
- **Delayed revenue.** What happens if your opening or expansion is delayed or you need to shut down temporarily for some reason? How long would it be before you ran out of cash?
- **Unforeseen costs.** What happens if the business has cost overruns or the cost of goods sold is higher than expected? Will you have enough money to pay the bills?

Operational risks. These risks affect your company's ability to function day to day in providing your products and services to your customers. Here are some examples:

- **Technology malfunctions.** Does the business rely on a computer system to process orders? If so, what would happen if your computer system crashed? How can you protect yourself from losing valuable files?
- **Cannibalization of operations.** Will one product or revenue stream take business away from another stream? For example, Argosy's component stream could compete with its home theater stream.
- **Capacity.** Will there be enough office or warehouse space if your business really takes off?

Competitive risks. These risks can be particularly unpredictable.

- **Pricing.** What if a competitor lowers its pricing to put you out of business?
- **Poaching.** What if a competitor tries or succeeds in hiring away your best people? What if your top salesperson quits and starts a competing shop?
- **Big competition.** What if a huge multinational competitor comes into the neighborhood?
- **New technology.** Imagine that your competitor develops new technology; what would it be, and how much business is it likely to cost you?

Organizational risks. These risks arise within your own company.

- **Key personnel.** What if some key personnel quit?
- **Partner problems.** What if partners or associates aren't pulling their weight? What if they're making employees unhappy?
- **Growth.** Can your organization deal with accelerated growth? Do you have a plan in place to handle a boom in customer demand?

- **Security.** What if an employee steals cash, data, or trade secrets?

Personal Risks

These risks affect you personally, aside from the business itself.

Opportunity risks have to do with closing off other outlets for your time and money. Starting and growing a company does not allow time for much else, but later you may wonder if the business really represents the best investment of your resources and energies.

- **Second-guessing.** What if you begin to second-guess your decision to throw yourself into the business? How will those doubts affect morale?
- **Lost opportunities.** What if a better opportunity comes along? Are you locked in? How will you handle any regrets or frustrations?
- **Acting out of desperation.** Are you starting this business under duress because you've lost money or are unable to find a satisfactory job? Is it possible you're just desperate to hang your hat on something?

Personal wealth risks threaten your earning potential and ability to create future wealth.

- **Inadequate upside.** Can your business eventually provide you with the financial security you need, or do you risk failing to meet your needs even if you succeed?
- **Failure.** What happens to you and your family if the business fails and you lose your entire investment? Will your family be able to tolerate your projected decline in its standard of living?

Relationship risks concern your interactions with family, friends, and associates. Don't shy away from these potential problems. Discuss issues with your partner. Talk about how the business might change your life. Try to arrive at a mutual understanding about travel demands and other effects the venture might have on your family life. Remember: Growing your business *successfully* can create plenty of stress of its own.

- **Workload.** Are you accurately gauging your workload and time commitment and their effects?
- **Pressure.** Do you have a support system strong enough to help you when times are tough?
- **Family fallout.** How would your family deal with the disappointment of a failed business? What about the finger-pointing that might follow? If you're considering a family-owned business, will spending day and night together become a strain?

External Risks

Governmental risks are especially unpredictable and far-reaching. What will happen to your business if the government enacts laws or regulations that affect it? I once helped develop strategy for a New York data company that compiled and sold lists of consumer names to businesses for use in advertising or marketing. Then Congress passed federal privacy legislation that crippled the business, resulting in an immediate 30 percent loss of income.

- **Legislation.** Is any legislation in the works that might harm the business?
- **Politics.** How would the company fare in a different presidential administration?
- **International.** What would happen to your business should the U.S. go to war or become embroiled in a prolonged international, financial, or political crisis?

Economic risks stem from the ebb and flow of financial conditions.

- **Buying power.** What happens if the economy plummets?

- **Dollar strength.** What happens if the relative value of the dollar increases or decreases?
- **Travel and entertainment.** What happens if airlines raise fares or hotels increase rates? How will your business suffer if you can't visit clients as often?
- **Labor unrest.** What happens if the trucking companies go on strike? The overnight delivery companies? The city workers' unions?

Not all dangers come with warning signs.

Environmental risks include the weather, which can play a bigger role than you might imagine. One of my previous businesses, for example, produced and distributed more than fifty million small booklets each year. One year, heavy rains struck the Northwest, which meant that the paper mills there couldn't create the pulp needed to make paper. The next year, paper was in such short supply that its price skyrocketed 30 percent and hit our profits hard.

- **Cost of goods.** Will any part of my business, including the cost of goods, be affected by the weather?
- **Seasonality.** Will my business function better or worse during different times of the year? If the business is seasonal, is there enough money to operate the business during the off-peak months?

Kaplan's Risk Assessment Matrix

After you've identified as many potential risks as you can, start thinking about how you might eliminate, minimize, or otherwise respond to each of them. The Kaplan Risk Assessment Matrix will give you an overview and serve as a useful reference as you execute your battle plan. It's a simple form, one that you can easily construct on a legal tablet or blank paper. On pages 54–55 is an example of what a completed one might look like.

Because the responses you provide for this matrix will also figure in the Business Assessment Model in the next chapter, it's important that you complete the entire matrix. If you omit risk areas, the model may not be accurate.

Rating your risk. Rate each risk on the following five-point scale, basing your rating on the likelihood of the risk occurring and the negative impact it would have on your business:

1. Severe risk that could cripple the business

2. Risk that would set the business back a bit but wouldn't destroy it

3. Moderate risk that would be more of a nuisance than anything

4. Unlikely risk that, should it become a reality, wouldn't hurt the business in any material way

5. No foreseeable risk at all or risk doesn't apply to your business

For each risk, note also on the risk matrix whether you have any control over the risk becoming a reality. Write a plan to mitigate each risk you can control and a contingency plan for those you can't.

After you have completed this matrix, you should review it from several perspectives:

Individually. Review each risk factor to see which ones rate a 3 or worse. You will need to pay greater attention to these. Make sure to develop solid plans should the risks rated 1 or 2 materialize.

By subgroup. Look at the makeup of each group. For example, consider business risk separately based on its financial, operational, competitive, and organizational elements. Averaging subgroup ratings will allow you to recognize which aspects of your endeavor are the riskiest.

Risky Business

What kinds of risks should you take? When should you take them? My answers are as follows: "as few as possible" and "as seldom as possible." When I do take risks, I try to make them calculated risks. After looking at the upside of opportunities, I focus much more energy on the downside. I ask, "What can

Kaplan's Risk Assessment Matrix

Risk Category	Rating	Control	No Control	Plan
BUSINESS RISKS				
Financial Issues				
Missed sales targets	4	X		Adjust staffing. Sales reporting to alert.
Late payments	3	X		Streamline invoicing.
Delayed revenue	3		X	Use bank credit line.
Unforeseen costs	3		X	Switch to daily reporting to alert. Set spending thresholds.
Operational Issues				
Technological malfunction	2	X		Run system checks. Back up data nightly.
Cannibalization of operations	3	X		Monitor product sales. Institute separate sales force if needed.
Capacity	3	X		Add clause in lease to allow for expansion.
Competitive Issues				
Pricing	3		X	Monitor competitor.
Poaching	2	X	X	Develop employee programs.
Big competition	2		X	Focus on service.
New technology	2	X		Automate.
Organizational Issues				
Key personnel	3	X	X	Develop employee programs.
Partner problems	4	X		Draw up operating agreements. Initiate performance-based compensation.
Growth	2	X		Process upgrades.
Security	3	X	X	Find backups. Develop security procedures.

Risk Category	Rating	Control	No Control	Plan
PERSONAL RISKS				
Opportunity Issues				
Second-guessing	3	X		Consider potential upside.
Lost opportunities	4		X	Negotiate out-clause in employment agreement.
Acting out of desperation	4	X		No contingency.
Personal Wealth Issues				
Weighing the downside	3	X		Wealth is a possibility if the business is successful.
Failure	4	X		Downsize automobile. Hold off on buying new home.
Relationship Issues				
Workload	2	X	X	Ask in-laws to help with kids.
Pressure	3	X	X	Network for back-up employment. Talk with spouse about going back to work.
Family fallout	3	X	X	Managed such problems before. Integrate family with workplace.
EXTERNAL RISKS				
Governmental Issues				
Legislation	2		X	Monitor via the web.
Politics	4		X	No contingency.
International	3		X	Unsure.
Economic Issues				
Buying power	2		X	If discretionary spending declines, reduce prices.
Dollar strength	4		X	Same as above.
Travel/entertainment	4		X	Reduce activity.
Labor unrest	3		X	Monitor transportation strike. Set up alternative distribution system.
Environmental Issues				
Cost of goods	4		X	Low risk—no plan.
Seasonality	3		X	Develop off-season items.

I do to eliminate or minimize my downside?" I always want to be sure I can live with the worst-case scenario.

This analysis is largely subjective, because each of us looks at potential downsides differently. For example, imagine you have a great opportunity to start a business with unlimited potential, but you'd have to move to an under-developed country to do so. If you were single with no children, you might look at this as a terrific learning experience, a chance to make it big—at worst, an adventure. If you were married with small children, however, you'd probably consider the downside unacceptable because, among other factors, schools and health care would be significant considerations.

> **Identifying potential risks can lead to actions that will eliminate or neutralize risks—or even turn them into opportunities.**

When you're faced with decisions entailing risk, always remember not to get carried away by the upside potential. Set aside plenty of time to assess the risks as well. Identifying potential risks can lead to actions that will eliminate or neutralize risks—or even turn them into opportunities. The point isn't to dwell on doom-and-gloom scenarios, but to implement two truths. First, the best way to maximize upside potential is to minimize the downside. Second, specific risks are often easier to calculate and manage than such upside intangibles as consumer mood and product appeal.

How's
Your Health?

W e're now nearing the payoff for the work you've done in part II. If you've followed the instructions and guidelines conscientiously, you've got the information you need to complete the analysis by assessing the current state and health of your business and its ability to handle growth.

Over the past fifteen years I have conducted this kind of analysis for more than one hundred businesses. I've distilled the essence of that experience to create my Business Assessment Model (BAM), which is the heart of this chapter.

The BAM uses twenty-five questions to assess how successful a new or existing business can be based on the solidity and stability of its foundation. It translates numerical information, assumptions, and risk—as well as the owner's personality, passion, and experience—into point values. Tabulated, these numbers add up to a Business Success Quotient (BSQ) that predicts the likelihood a company will succeed. If the BSQ is unfavorable, identifying and correcting weaknesses revealed by the BAM can help reshape the business.

You can see that the BAM is not just dry numbers. One of its beauties is that even though it's based mostly on objective measures and not on emotions or hunches, it does take into account such intangibles as the owner's character and commitment to the business.

Rating Your Foundation

Complete the worksheet below by writing your score for each question on the line provided. At the end of each financial question, I refer to the subject matter covered earlier so you can go back and review it. (You may want to photocopy the pages below or visit **www.differencemaker.com,** click "Freebies," then click "Calculators.")

When you're finished, add up your scores to get your BSQ. To learn the potential success of your business model, match your BSQ with its point range located at the end of the worksheet.

Regardless of your score, review every question on which you got less than the best possible score. Try to retool your business to maximize your score for that question.

Assumptions and Preparation

1. How did you determine your numbers and
assumptions?   _____

- I haven't yet created official assumptions or projections. **0 pts.**
- I created assumptions and reports off the top of my head without any input from others. **4 pts.**
- I created assumptions and had them reviewed by a peer. **7 pts.**
- I created assumptions with input from others and used an accountant to develop or review my financial projections. **15 pts.**

2. Did you discount your revenue projection
by at least 10 percent?   _____

- No. **0 pts.**
- Yes. **5 pts.**

3. Did you create a detailed organizational chart complete with job descriptions and salaries? _____

- I haven't created one. **0 pts.**
- I created one but omitted either descriptions or salaries. **5 pts.**
- I created a chart, complete with job descriptions and salaries. **10 pts.**

Numbers

4. Did you analyze each revenue stream to determine new ways to increase the revenues in each one? Did you make someone in your company accountable for the success of each revenue stream and key part of their compensation to their results? **(Projected Revenue Statement, Revenue opportunities)** _____

- No. **0 pts.**
- I analyzed the revenue streams but didn't assign accountability to any of them. **5 pts.**
- I analyzed the revenue streams, assigned accountability to some, but have not implemented performance-based compensation. **10 pts.**
- I analyzed the revenue streams, assigned accountability for each one, and implemented performance-based compensation. **15 pts.**

5. Over the course of the first twelve months, does your company have enough cash flow to pay its bills? That is, are the numbers on the cumulative cash flow line all positive? **(Projected Cash Flow Statement, Cumulative cash flow)** _____

- No. **0 pts.**
- Yes. **10 pts.**

6. When will you have your long-term debt paid off? **(Projected Balance Sheet, How much debt will the business have?)** _____

- Longer than 7 years. **–2 pts.**
- Within 7 years. **0 pts.**

- Within 4–6 years. **2 pts.**
- Within 3 years. **4 pts.**
- Within 2 years. **6 pts.**
- Within 1 year. **8 pts.**
- No long-term debt. **10 pts.**

7. When can you begin to take money other than a reasonable salary out of the business? **(Projected Cash Flow Statement, Cash available for reinvestment or distribution)** _____

- 5 years or longer. **0 pts.**
- After year 4. **1 pt.**
- 3–4 years. **2 pts.**
- 1–2 years. **7 pts.**
- 6 months–1 year. **8 pts.**
- Earlier than 6 months. **10 pts.**

8. Over the next five years, the percentages of operating expenses to sales: **(Income statement, Operating expenses)** _____

- Increase through the years. **0 pts.**
- Remain flat through the years. **2 pts.**
- Remain flat for 2 years, then decrease. **6 pts.**
- Decrease through the years. **10 pts.**

9. In reviewing the projected net income dollar figure, growth in years 1–4: **(Projected Income [Profit/Loss] Statement)** _____

- Falls short of my expectations, but the business will find a way to make more. **0 pts.**
- Meets my expectations. **6 pts.**
- Exceeds my expectations by 25–49 percent. **8 pts.**
- Exceeds my expectations by 50+ percent. **10 pts.**

10. What is the projected current ratio of your business? **(Projected Balance Sheet, Can your business pay its debts?)** _____

- Less than 0.75:1. **–10 pts.**

- Between 0.76:1 and 0.99:1. **–3 pts**.
- 1:1. **3 pts.**
- Between 1:1 and 1.49:1. **5 pts**.
- Between 1.5:1 and 1.9:1. **8 pts**.
- 2:0 or higher. **10 pts.**

Risk

For each of the following areas, list the average group risk rating you determined when completing the risk matrix found in the previous chapter **(Kaplan's Risk Assessment Matrix)**. Indicate the level of risk, using the same 1–5 scale you used for the risk matrix.

11. Business: Financial   _____

12. Business: Operational   _____

13. Business: Competitive   _____

14. Business: Organizational   _____

15. Personal: Opportunity   _____

16. Personal: Wealth   _____

17. Personal: Relationship   _____

18. External: Governmental   _____

19. External: Economic   _____

20. External: Environmental   _____

Experience and Style

21. What experience do you or your partner have in business?   _____

- Never owned a business. **0 pts.**
- Owned one business, moderate success. **5 pts.**
- Owned one business, large success. **8 pts.**
- Owned two successful businesses. **9 pts.**

22. How long have you worked in the industry?   _____

- Never. **0 pts.**
- Less than 1 year in a lower-level capacity. **3 pts.**
- 1–2 years, middle management or sales. **6 pts.**
- 3–5 years, middle management. **8 pts.**
- 5+ years in a management capacity. **10 pts.**

23. What is your management style? _____

- I blindly delegate everything and operate totally hands-off. **0 pts.**
- I feel that I must do everything, because if I don't do it, it won't get done. **4 pts.**
- I listen to input from others but seldom take their advice. **6 pts.**
- Once my employees have proven themselves, I delegate with controls. **8 pts.**

24. How many hours per week are you accustomed to working? _____

- As little as possible. **0 pts.**
- 40 hours per week. **5 pts.**
- Some overtime. **5 pts.**
- Whatever it takes. **8 pts.**

25. Are you focusing 100 percent of your work effort on this business? _____

- No. **0 pts.**
- Yes. **10 pts.**

Business Success Quotient

Total from all 25 questions above: _____

Key

185–200 Your business foundation is solid and you appear to have a healthy business. The assumptions, numbers, and risk levels all support success. Your current business model is on course, and solid execution of your growth plan should follow. Good luck!

160–184 Your business growth idea is viable and you

should proceed. To ensure that you're operating with the best chance for success, you need to work on your assumptions, numbers, or risk levels. Revisit your projections and business model and try to raise your score to the 185–200 level.

140–159 This business is on the threshold of viability. Most businesses fall in this range. The numbers, assumptions, or risk levels are out of the norm for a healthy business and are probably dragging down your score. Revisit the questions on which you scored low and try to reshape your business to get it on a better track. Don't let up until your score hits at least 160—but shoot for 185. After that, monitor your business carefully to make sure the actual numbers are in line with your projections. Failure to do so could be fatal to the business.

120–139 This business foundation does not currently meet the criteria for viability and will probably not make it. The business is performing below standards in too many areas. If you have your heart set on this business, you have some work to do—starting now. You'll need to reshape or overhaul much of your business model in order to move your score into the acceptable range.

119 or less This is a very high-risk business and is not likely to work. If the business model doesn't change significantly, and quickly, this enterprise will probably go out of business within a year. You should seriously consider moving on to a different opportunity.

Once you've boosted your score into the upper ranges, your business will be on track for success. But your work has only begun. It's time to move on to even more pressing issues: identifying strategies to grow your business.

Part III
THE ROLE OF SALES

"Since salespeople are on the front lines
in contacting customers, they should know more
than anyone else about what customers need."

The Cornerstone
of Growth

I n the many businesses I've worked with over the years, most of the growth has stemmed from sales. Fascinating, Steve. How about telling us something we don't know? Okay, let me explain. I'm not talking about growing simply by pushing to sell more of your current offerings. I'm talking about the central role that the sales function needs to fill throughout the whole process of expanding your business—that is, both the development and selling of new products and services.

Nor am I saying that the sales organization can take the place of solid strategy and planning; however, sales can and should play a vital part in the process. In thinking ahead, in sniffing out opportunities, in planning for new products, services, and markets, a good sales team is your eyes, ears, and nose. Salespeople should go everywhere and talk to everyone. Who better to do the forward reconnaissance for your organization?

Sales Responsibility and Opportunity

In planning and carrying out an effective and systematic growth strategy, regardless of the size of your company or your sales department, pay particular attention to the sales department and the relationships between salespeople and customers. When I was experiencing some of my first company's most explosive growth, I had a sales force of exactly three—including myself. As the owner, in addition to running the company, I was bringing in about 80 percent of the sales, and that's not an uncommon ratio for a small business.

Five Principles for Sales Success

1. Do your homework.

2. Anticipate customer needs.

3. Expand your network.

4. Increase commissions.

5. Develop your talent.

Understanding the following principles will help establish a sales culture in your business that will foster maximum successful growth. Every person in your sales organization should read this book in its entirety—but at a minimum, this chapter and the next two. And by "every person in your sales organization," I mean everyone who comes in contact or communicates with the customer, not just those who meet customers with an order pad in hand. People who deal with customers in any way can have an effect on sales, and all those whose actions can impact current or future sales—sales staff, account managers, customer service representatives, shipping clerks, complaint department staff, and so on—are effectively part of your sales organization.

As you and your sales staff read through the principles and procedures outlined in this and later chapters, keep the big picture in mind. Some of the ideas will apply more than others to your situation; use them to think beyond what you routinely do to bring in revenue. Let them lead you to fresh ideas about what you're selling, and to whom.

1. Do your homework. Before you seek information from customers, learn as much as you can about industry trends so you can ask informed, intelligent questions. Look

An Appetite for Success

Yum!™ brands is the largest owner of restaurants in the world, with such flagship names as Taco Bell, Pizza Hut, KFC, A&W, and Long John Silver's. If you visit Yum!'s website at **www.yum.com,** you can't help noticing where this company is going. Yum! is focusing much of its future growth on the Asian market, specifically China. This makes sense, because China has the huge potential customer numbers to fill Yum!'s fast-food restaurants to capacity. The important thing here isn't necessarily why Yum! is focusing on this market—rather, it's the fact that Yum! has made such a commitment to this market and is openly broadcasting it. When I browsed through Yum!'s website, Yum! was screaming with opportunity for any business that could help the company achieve its objectives in China.

As a salesperson or business owner, I'd have to ask myself how my products and services might be able to help Yum! in China. More specifically, I'd look for ways I might expand the scope of what I'm doing to capture some of this opportunity to work with Yum! Dan Johnson, an old friend and business associate of mine with experience in customer satisfaction research in the U.S., has sold millions of dollars' worth of research products in his career. We spent a lot of time thinking up ways to grow his business by applying in the China market the same techniques he has used in the U.S. to measure customer satisfaction. This might involve forming an alliance with a partner in China, which is challenging, but the upside could be massive profits. In today's global marketplace, providing services internationally is getting easier every day.

for facts, figures, and trends that will help you shape your product or service for the next round of sales effort. Use all available resources: online trend data, company websites, annual reports for public companies, demographics, industry publications, competitors, industry guides, trade shows, customer surveys, even a good walkabout in your own retail store. These sources will tell you about your customers' needs, raise your "partner IQ," and set the table for future business ideas.

Owner action: This one falls mostly on you, the owner, personally. You'll need to take the lead and authorize the development of any research. You'll also have to balance the flow of information with your actual need. Assign someone you trust to sift through the flood and dig out what's relevant.

Frankly, I always hated to see a ton of e-mail articles floating around the company, set adrift with the intention of educating the team, but serving mostly to distract them. Keep your team focused by making sure that the information shared is directly related to growing your business. Consider setting up a reconnaissance team that uses "homework" information as the basis for leads in new business opportunities. With an eye on your entire industry, explore how clients are using your products, and then seek information on ways to zero in on the biggest opportunities.

2. Anticipate customer needs. Regardless of whether you're involved in business-to-business or business-to-consumer sales, if you're going to sell as much as you can you'll need to develop strong, long-term relationships with your customers. The best way to do this is to anticipate what your customers need in order to be successful at whatever they are doing. Since salespeople are on the frontlines in contacting customers, they should know more than anyone else does about what customers need. Who better to come up with new products and services than those who know your customers best?

One of the first businesses I acquired was a business-to-business graphic arts company that was trying to expand by adding a new service, consumer promotions, to its line. I was working there as a salesman. The owners weren't in communication with the customers, so they didn't understand what customers actually wanted. I tried to tell them, but I was young and inexperienced and my ideas weren't taken seriously.

I noticed that the company was trying to sell many different promotions at the same time. The result was that no single promotion sold enough to make money. Even to a young sales guy, it seemed logical to focus on one or two promotions,

New from Old

This table outlines current products sold and potential new products generated from a customer needs assessment. Compare the two columns, item by item. Note how the proposed product or service relates to or dovetails with the existing offerings.

Current Product or Service	Proposed Product or Service
Gift baskets	Cards, delivery service
Day surgery clinics	Travel to home, postcare checkups, medicine
Residential real estate	School registration information, learning the new neighborhood, selling current residence, moving furnishings
Printing	Packaging, fulfillment services
Video rental	Snacks, pizza, delivery
Marketing consulting	Printing, mailing services, design
Tax preparation	Tax planning, estate planning, financial planning

sell them well, and turn a profit on them before adding more. But I couldn't get anybody in the company to listen to me.

Want to guess what happened? That's right, sales lagged and the owners ran into financial trouble.

I bought the business, made some simple and obvious changes—mainly, streamlining the sales effort to maximize profitability and selling what the customers truly wanted to buy. I hired more salespeople. Sales and profits soared, and this made everybody happy. I ended up selling this business for some pretty big bucks—all because I brought a salesperson's feet-on-the-ground perspective to the customers' needs.

So get out there and really talk to customers! Make it about more than just selling products and services—make it about the customers' success and happiness. The more you know your customers' needs, the better you can anticipate what they need to buy from your company. Ask your business customers about their short- and long-term initiatives; they will be happy to tell you. Listen as they explain problems they are having in particular areas. Can you be the solution?

Owner action: Support new business development internally, giving accolades and rewards for innovative product or service ideas. Consider mentions in company newsletters and at company meetings, along with other incentives.

3. Expand your network. As you are selling, work hard to branch out through your current customers. If you have many individual customers, get to know more about them after they purchase your products or services. Find out the names of those who are using them, how they are using them, and why. Do they use your product alone, or do they use it in conjunction with other products? If it's the latter, can you provide those other products as well?

If your customers are other businesses, try to work your way into the fabric of the customer's company by expanding your reach into other parts of it. Meet people in as many different departments and operational areas as possible—and not just other buyers. One of my most effective strategies was to find out about my customers' initiatives long before my competition did. I got this information from the many relationships I'd developed on the operational side of the businesses.

One of my customers was a packaged-goods company that distributed product samples such as shampoos and candy to various target markets, including young kids and teens. I had developed strong ties with operational departments—market research, distribution, public relations, and, yes, even purchasing—and my contacts would tell me when their company's new products were scheduled

Everyone you talk to will have something to say.

to be introduced. This information gave me a huge head start on my competition.

For example, if that customer was coming out with a new brand targeted at college students, this early knowledge would give me enough time to presell a sampling program—and to develop a network of universities and colleges to distribute the samples through. Had I heard about this new product initiative in the trade magazines or on the traditional customer communication timetable, it would have been too late for me to do anything at all. Not only would I not have had time to presell, I could never have even competed for the business in the first place, since I would not have had any colleges to sell or any time to build a network.

Owner action: Support communication. It's one thing to expect your employees to build solid relationships, but as the owner you'll need to put your money where your mouth is. Encourage your salespeople and operating people—everyone who

Selling Futures

I used to have a monthly contest for my salespeople to recognize innovative thinking that might result in the sale of a new product or service. Each salesperson would fill out an entry form describing the proposed product or service and the customer need it would fill. The salespeople had to analyze each new idea for relevance, pricing, and other criteria (but I kept the form simple so it wouldn't be burdensome). Actual sales were not required, but that was okay, since the objective was to keep the sales force thinking big and new and communicating with customers all the time. The winner received a trophy, to be displayed on her desk for a month, along with bragging rights. The incentives worked.

interacts with your customers—to go out there and spend time meeting customers. Monitor your team's progress by asking for debriefings: How did the meeting go? What do you anticipate the next step to be? Although it takes a bit of time to get into the heart of your customer, each meeting should produce a useful nugget of information.

If you have many customers on a one-to-one level, draw up a questionnaire of key information you need. Have your salespeople, cashiers, and other personnel gather the data incrementally by asking a question or two each time they meet a customer, being careful not to harass or interrogate.

4. Motivate sales. Whether you're trying to expand your business by promoting new products or services, or by going into new markets, it's especially important for your sales force to be extramotivated to sell (and especially presell) your new offerings. Few things are worse for your bottom line than a sales force that's just going through the motions. Salespeople need to care about your product or service. If they don't, that gets communicated, and the prospect wonders, Why should I care?

> **Few things are worse for your bottom line than a sales force that's just going through the motions.**

The sales force should never lack for motivation to succeed in a new business development arena. That's why it's important to give your salespeople incentives to help develop new products and services, as well as new customers.

When I was first starting out, I was a bit put off by salespeople who, it seemed to me, didn't care much about the business. Oh, they were eager enough to make their commissions, but whether they were selling BMWs or bagels, it was all the same to them. Show me the money! New products? Sure, we'll sell 'em as soon as we finish making our commissions on the tried-and-true stuff. We know we can make money on that.

Before long it occurred to me that the salespeople didn't care about risky new business because they didn't have any incentive. Risk was for business owners, not salespeople. So I decided to give them an incentive: a stake in the success of the new product or service. I tweaked the commission structure so that the sales force would benefit directly from the success of the new offerings that they had helped develop by keeping their eyes open, asking questions, and preselling.

Owner action: Give your sales force a stake in developing new business, whether through new markets or by offering new products or services. One way to accomplish this is by giving them—in addition to the standard commission on all sales—a percentage of the profits from the new business. With this incentive, they are more likely to make new products and services successful. It keeps them as concerned as management is about the financial health of the whole business. If they know that they can make money by helping launch a successful new service, they will put more effort into it. And if they know that an unsuccessful new-product launch can threaten the health of the company (and perhaps their jobs), they will pay extra attention.

Some managers treat sales as a kind of support service, separate from the main function, rather than as an integral part of the company. Their attitude is: We're the brains, we develop products, we do the math, we count the money; sales is just our pipeline to customers. This way of thinking about sales is a mistake, leading to missed opportunities for responding to changes and potential in the marketplace, and devaluing and possibly alienating the sales staff. Be responsive to the needs of your sales force. Get quotes to them quickly; show solidarity by visiting their big customers; pay commissions on time. The happier your sales force, the healthier your sales.

5. Develop your talent. As my businesses evolved, I needed smart people to run various departments. Many of my original employees, although young, had developed and grown the business and were best equipped to succeed in larger roles. In fact, most of my best department heads had been with me since the beginning, in entry-level positions. They had already shown me what they could do, so I assigned them to manage and grow their departments. Even some who had never attended college ended up running large divisions of the company and taking home upward of $350,000 annually.

> Most of my best department heads had been with me since the beginning, in entry-level positions.

Owner action: Promote internally. Don't be afraid to give opportunities to those at lower levels. Work with them as your company grows and give them the opportunity to rise to the occasion. I value heart and drive over degrees and diplomas, but that's a judgment call you'll have to make on your own.

Regardless of the number of employees you have, promoting internally is a huge motivator. You'll reap big productivity rewards from your employees, because they'll want to do a great job to prove their value to your company—and earn those big promotions.

The Rule of Go

W hen I was starting out with my first business, I spent my days selling to customers and my nights running the business. Among my duties was developing new products and services. I came up with several promising ideas and tried them out. Some were winners, big time. Others turned out to be nightmares. The problem was that the losers cost me more than the winners brought in, leaving me with a net loss—not only in money but in morale and momentum.

Obviously, I couldn't keep going down that road. I needed some way to determine in advance which ideas were moneymakers and which were cash sinkholes. That would be useful knowledge, to say the least.

I went back and reviewed all the new product and service ideas I had tried, the ones that had worked and the ones that had tanked. Was there a common factor in either group? The strategies were different in so many ways that at first it was hard to find a pattern.

Then I saw it: The ideas that had worked were those I had discussed in advance with my customers. When I had presented the idea, obtained the customer's input on its utility and effectiveness, and asked for a commitment to buy, the outcome had always been successful.

In a word: Duh!

They were already customers. I knew how they operated, how they bought, and what they needed. I knew which ones I could count on, the ones who would follow through when they committed to something. And they knew me. They were accustomed to dealing with me. They knew they could trust me. When it came to developing new products and services, the relationship we'd formed, and the information coming out of it, turned out to be far more valuable to me than spending a lot of money on market research or going by gut instinct.

This realization opened my eyes to the role that sales plays in new business development—not just at the end, where the sale is made, but at the beginning and throughout the new-business development cycle. That's when I created the rule that now guides my business growth decisions, a rule that has saved me from nightmares.

> **Rule of Go: If a new product, service, or concept can't be presold to customers, it should not be developed or introduced to the market-place. If it can, then it's a GO!**

I call it the **Rule of Go**: If a new product, service, or concept can't be presold to customers, it should not be developed or introduced to the marketplace. If it can, then it's a GO!

Since I began following the Rule of Go, I haven't had a single new-product or new-service failure in more than fifty tries. Quite a track record, right? That's what comes from getting beat up early and often. You learn the right way to do things. And in this case, the right way is not so mysterious, because when you think about it, it makes perfect sense. The idea is simple, and it comes in two parts:

1. Every new product or service should directly meet a specific need of the customer.

2. Preselling minimizes the risk of failure.

Preselling is perhaps the most critical component in the successful development and marketing of new products and services. No matter how great an idea your new product or service seems to you, if you can't presell it to its intended customers, it's a high-risk long shot and should be scrapped.

Nothing could be simpler.

Setting Up for a Slam Dunk

If you presell effectively, you should be able to

- minimize the risks associated with growth,
- guarantee sales by getting a signed contract before developing your new product or service, and
- ensure profitability by getting development expenses paid by current or new customers.

So, what, exactly, is preselling? How is it different from just selling? It's like this: When you're selling, you're going to a prospective customer and saying, in effect, "Here's what we sell. We've been selling this product to other customers for two years now. It's a tested, proven product. It's rated excellent; our customers are happy with it, and here are some testimonials to prove it."

Easy enough, right? Now, here's what you're saying when you're preselling: "We're planning to develop a product that we feel will help you meet your initiatives [either they've told you their needs or you've figured it out yourself] and increase your profits. It will be available in two months. Meanwhile, we need to sign a contract with you to supply this product when it's ready to distribute—and oh, yeah, we'd like you to help us pay for its development."

Think about it. You're going to an existing customer and asking for a commitment to buy something you can't deliver immediately, and, perhaps, help you develop it, too. Interesting challenge, right? I can hear you shouting now, "No way!"

When you're preselling to an existing customer, you've got a degree of credibility from the start.

But it's not impossible. In fact, it's pretty routine. First off, if you're an established business, you have customers. When you're preselling to an existing customer, you've got a degree of credibility from the start. You've already made the first, maybe the most important, part of the sale: getting the customer to trust you. This gives you a leg up on your competitors, even those with existing products you might be gearing up to compete with. Need help with development?

Cleaning Up

Most of the clients of my first marketing-and-promotion company came from the packaged goods industry: toothpaste, laundry detergent, food, and other products. These customers paid us to distribute special offers and promotional materials to their target markets, which ranged from kids and teens to college students and a variety of adult groups. We reached these people through such venues as schools, colleges, and doctors' offices.

One fine day, we brainstormed ways of expanding our business by broadening our marketing demographics. We were already reaching families with kids in elementary school; could we grow by expanding our existing customer base? We considered many strategies. Some were way out there, as should be the case when brainstorming, but others seemed promising.

We narrowed the most likely strategies to (1) targeting parents with kids 2–5 years old who were entering day care or preschool, (2) marketing similar products and samples to adults 21–45 through health clubs, and (3) offering our sampling programs to English as a Second Language classes for immigrants of all ages. After due consideration, we rated the first idea the best of the lot. With the younger age bracket, we could build on our current target market and get more business from current customers, along with some new ones.

The goal now was simple: to find at least one current customer who liked the idea enough to sign a contract with us before we invested money in it. We, in turn, would give them category exclusivity for the products they wanted to include in the program. This meant that, in exchange for committing to us early, they could lock out their competition.

Proctor & Gamble's Tide detergent was one of our oldest customers. We were distributing samples and materials to Tide's main market: families with children. Our focus had been on 6- to 12-year-olds. Parents with kids aged 2–5 have different laundry needs than those with kids aged 0–2 and 6–12. Based on the good results Tide had had with us over several years and the strong relationship we had built with them, would they agree to let us address other family market segments with new products?

Tide loved the idea. The company enjoyed working with us and—most important—knew that we could deliver on our promises. This was the foundation for our growth strategy. Because of Tide's participation, we were able to reduce all financial risk for the new product and guarantee a profit on it before we spent a single penny.

Think of a current customer as a kind of a partner—a partner with both motivation and money.

If you're properly managing your customer relationships, providing effective service, and meeting their standards of quality, you're well on your way. Now it's time for them to show you just how much they appreciate you by signing up for your next venture—*now!*

Six Gotta-Do's

Let's say you've done the cost and feasibility analyses necessary to make sure your strategy is workable and profitable. Now you can start the presell. Here are six things to do when preselling customers:

1. Select your target. Knowing which customers to target for the presell isn't always as simple as it may appear. Now, if you're implementing an idea that came straight from a customer, this step takes care of itself because the customer is, in effect, self-selected and you're developing a growth strategy based on the customer's specific needs. Otherwise, the following questions about your customers should start you down the right path:

- **Which customers do you have the longest relationships with?** Since these customers have the most experience with your company, they are good candidates for a presell.
- **Which customers are spending the most money with you?** Money talks. If they're spending money on item A, they might be able to buy item B as well.
- **Which customers impact other customers?** If your customer is a business, then who inside the business can navigate the bureaucracy to make things happen, such as getting a go-ahead on a new product idea? If your customers are individuals, then who among them has the most influence over others? Are any of them members of clubs or other groups or organizations that might help spread the word like a virus?

A Case for the Presell

Robinson & Mullock Associates is a law firm specializing in immigration and criminal defense law, with a client base mostly of Eastern Europeans. Having cornered the market in immigration and criminal law in Philadelphia, Michael Robinson and Samuel Mullock decided it was time to grow their business. They looked at their strengths and listed four factors as the ones contributing the most to their success: (1) connections at the State Attorney's Office, (2) knowledge of the Eastern European client, (3) a solid, captive client base of loyal client families providing the bulk of their profits, and (4) development of processes that allowed them to standardize their work and complete it quickly and effectively.

As is typical in partnerships, the two had different ideas about which growth strategy to pursue. Mike wanted to add two services (business and real estate law) to the current product mix; Sam wanted to expand to the Hispanic market, a rapidly growing segment of the population. After a few passionate pleas, Mike yielded and Sam set off to conquer the Hispanic marketplace on behalf of the firm.

A few months down the road and a chunk of cash later, things weren't happening as planned. Money spent on advertising, marketing, and bilingual personnel disappeared into the black hole of customer indifference. Mike and Sam bailed out of their Hispanic expansion strategy.

How did Robinson & Mullock miss the boat?

- They forgot the most important rule in business growth—the Rule of Go: Presell, presell, presell. Had they tried, they would have encountered the obstacles early and not spent so much money. Like most business owners, Sam simply decided to focus on something new, fell in love with an idea, and threw money into start-up and implementation.

- They had an established, loyal clientele, Eastern Europeans, to whom it would have been easy, and much less expensive, to presell additional services such as real estate or business law before adding that expertise to the firm.

- They let ego cloud their business judgment—a common but potentially deadly mistake.

2. Identify the need. Know what your customers are thinking and where they are going next. If your customer is a business, find out what its various departments are focusing on for the next year or so. If your customers are individuals, study their buying history. What have they bought from you? When? How often? What do they use your product or service for? What other products have they bought from you?

3. Attack the need. Position the product or service you wish to presell to fill the customer's specific needs (which, of course, you know—either because the customer told you explicitly or because, given your experience with that customer, you have a high degree of certainty). It's one thing to have a good idea and try to sell it based on your relationship and your company's performance; it's another thing entirely to have your track record to lean on when you're showing them exactly why your product or service fits their future needs.

4. Answer the "Why us?" question. Offer your customer a reason to say yes, such as, "You're such a great customer that we wanted you to have first crack at this." Also consider benefits such as exclusivity or customization of the new product to best fit the customer's specific needs.

5. Prepare sales materials. This is a judgment call. My rule of thumb: Spend only what's needed to make the presale. If the customer is covering only the development costs, or if you wish to sell more of this product or service to others, you can spend more later if necessary. Sales materials can get expensive and quickly become outdated—and besides, in the presell, the customer is buying based on your reputation and its experience with you, not on materials.

> **Once a customer commits, you can go full-out and start spending more on something you know is going to be a winner.**

I've made many presales of $10 million or more using only a two-page typed proposal. The proposal was well written and had all the necessary details, of course, but my point is that you don't need to go crazy here. Remember, it's *you and your business* the customer is buying, not a stack of paper or a fancy brochure.

Effective Business Proposals

To maximize your chances of preselling your product or service:

- Submit your proposal in the format your prospect prefers.

  Include the following essential information:

  Strategic fit. Why is your product or service the right fit for the customer? Ideally, use information gleaned from the prospect.

  Products or services to be provided. What do you want the prospect to buy from you?

  Pricing. What will you charge? Include cost analysis or other information, if relevant, to justify the price.

  Timing. Which critical items are needed, and when?

  Contact information. Who is the contact at your company in case the proposal is passed to others?

- Use the prospect's terms and language. This will position you as an insider. Listen to everything that's said when inside the prospect's business.

- Submit your proposal without delay.

- Archive successful proposals electronically as templates for future proposals.

Whenever the proposed new product or service was in a different genre from what I was currently selling the customer, which was often the case, I'd need to go a step further. If, for example, I was selling marketing programs but then shifted to something very different, such as packaging material, I'd provide some artwork, along with samples of the material I wanted to use for the packaging. But even then, I didn't go crazy spending money.

Here's the point: You don't necessarily have to pop for the big bucks for make-ready manufacturing or to get actual manufactured samples made. I find that nice comps or computer-generated creative work fine. Often potential suppliers are happy to give you samples or even make up comps for you at their expense. There are also many great software programs that you can use to easily create quality materials for the presell. Once a customer commits, you can go full-out and start spending more on something you know is going to be a winner.

6. Get the sale. The key to preselling, as opposed to simply seeking customers' interest or a "maybe I'll buy," is that preselling eliminates the "nice factor"—that is, customers humoring you by telling you that your idea is good, just to avoid hurting your feelings. Preselling involves commitment on your part to developing and offering the product or service for sale, and it involves commitment on the customer's part to buying the product or service once it becomes reality.

Here's an important point to remember: Preselling is a flexible concept. The minimum commitment you ask from the customer is whatever it takes to eliminate your risk, or at least make it manageable. The degree of commitment depends on the size of your business, the nature of your product or service, the cost of developing and manufacturing, the risk to your company, and many other factors. You may ask the customer to cover the development costs, or, if the cost of manufacturing the product or providing the service is high, ask for a minimum sales amount with development costs built in.

Preselling is tough, but absolutely essential.

Preselling is not for the fainthearted; it can be a real high-wire act, a delicate balance of the vendor's and customer's interests that requires a mutual show of good faith. Your customer may well be reluctant to provide funding or to commit to a sale on speculation. Customers must weigh

1. their own perceived risk, and
2. the amount of funding they would have to commit against
   a. their projected need for your proposed product or service,
   b. the extra profits they might realize if your new product or service fulfills its promise,
   c. your track record with the company, and
   d. other factors such as any additional benefits you've promised them in your presell in exchange for their commitment.

You are, naturally, just as reluctant (or more so, depending on your relative size) to plunge into debt on a verbal commitment to buy. That's why you need to get that signature. If you simply cannot, you must weigh the time and money you must invest in development and production, the loss of other opportunities to sell existing products or services to current customers, and the danger of losing a good customer if the product or service does not live up to expectations. Then you have to compare those risks with the opportunity to open up new revenue streams and multiply your profitability, the possibility of gaining a new set or class of customers, a big commission, and the chance to grow from a small, client-dependent business to a market-driving Elephant.

> **Remember: Intention to buy is nothing. Presell, presell, presell—and get that signature.**

Remember: Intention to buy is nothing. Presell, presell, presell—and get that signature.

Inside or Outside the Family?

T he folks at Eden Day Spa were doing good business. Their appointment book was filled with upscale customers who were enjoying a variety of massages, facials, and other beauty treatments. The six full-time massage therapists and four full-time manicurists, pedicurists, and other beauty specialists were booked to more than 80 percent capacity. Business was going so well that the owners, Madison and Jerry Cooper, decided it was time to expand.

There were many ways to accomplish this, including the obvious one: Hire more specialists. Instead, they chose to expand by adding a tanning service to their offerings. Tanning facilities were popping up all over town, and there were quite a lot of stories in the news about the negative effects of direct sunlight. It seemed like an easy win.

The Coopers figured that adding tanning beds would allow them to

- squeeze more dollars from their current core customers,
- gain some new customers who would sign up just for the tanning, and

- cross-sell between the tanning and the current spa services.

However, it wasn't long after they'd installed the beautiful, state-of-the-art tanning beds that they knew they'd been burned.

Hardly any of their spa customers signed up for the tanning services. In fact, after three solid weeks of promoting memberships, Eden had converted only three spa customers to the new tanning service. The Sun Tan Only membership drive wasn't doing that much better, and the costs of the tanning service quickly began to erode the profits from their other spa services.

> **The owners had not bothered to test their idea before investing in it—a must, whether their strategy was developed internally or externally.**

As if that weren't bad enough, the tanning customers were a much younger and less affluent market segment. This demographic began to affect the culture of the spa—a potential death sentence for a business offering such personal services. Unless something was done quickly to keep its wealthier customers from moving to another spa, the business was doomed.

So Madison and Jerry bit the bullet after only two months and got out of the tanning business. The financial damages were significant—the cost of the beds and other supplies, the electrical upgrades needed to support the machines, the marketing materials, and more—but a lot less than the cost of losing the business.

Rubbed the Wrong Way

What happened? On paper, it had looked great. Tanning salons were doing a booming business everywhere, and the fit was promising. Eden Day Spa was a beauty salon, and didn't most people think tan was beautiful? Surely, if they had been asked, customers would have agreed.

But they were not asked. The idea did not come from the customers, it came from the owners of Eden Day Spa, and the owners had not bothered to test their idea before investing in it—a must, regardless of whether their strategy was developed internally or externally. If they had asked customers what they wanted, the answer might have been dermabrasion or waxing or Botox or aromatherapy or any of a multitude of things. If they had asked about tanning beds, they might have heard a few customers say no, that's for the youngsters, the iPod crowd; we prefer the French Riviera and real sun.

> **Some of the smartest decisions we make are the things we decide *not* to do.**

The Coopers compounded their error by failing to gain an understanding of who they were selling to. An inexpensive survey of customers, along with some elementary observations (How much did the customers spend each week? What kind of cars did they drive? Did they wear expensive clothes and jewelry?), would have revealed the danger the owners were facing. Their current clientele did not fit the demographics of those who went to tanning salons.

Move forward but watch where you step.

The Rule of Go could have offered the Coopers some protection, especially since converting their current spa customers into tanning customers was such an important part of their success strategy. Compounding their mistake of implementing an idea that originated *inside* the company, they didn't even test the waters by trying to presell their tanning packages to existing customers. If they had, they would have realized that tanning was doomed to fail.

Remember: Some of the smartest decisions we make are the things we decide *not* to do.

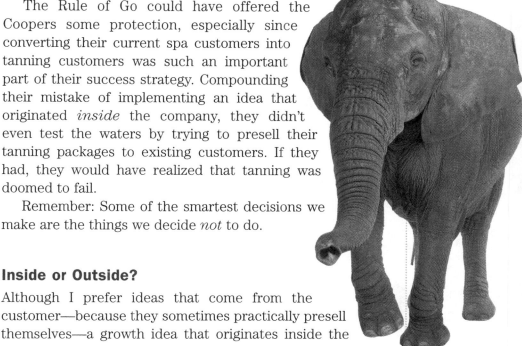

Inside or Outside?

Although I prefer ideas that come from the customer—because they sometimes practically presell themselves—a growth idea that originates inside the

Internally Driven Growth

Advantages

- Growth based on company core expertise
- Easier to plan
- More passion about the idea
- Easier to pull the trigger because it's your idea

Disadvantages

- Preselling more difficult
- Materials needed for preselling or selling cost more
- Risk of failure higher than with external growth ideas
- Difficult to be objective

Externally Driven Growth

Advantages

- Success rate much higher than with internal development
- Customer more likely to fund your growth
- High potential for new areas of growth and new revenue streams across many industries and markets

Disadvantages

- Heavy reliance on sales force and customer relationships to discover customer needs and plans
- Requires ability to navigate customer's bureaucracy
- Extra cost of incentives for sales staff

business can also be used effectively if you know your customers and your market, diligently analyze all the factors, and make a special effort to presell it.

Internally driven growth is growth based on an idea that originates within the provider company: a new product, a new service that meshes with a currently provided service, or a plan to expand existing markets to new types of customers or new geographic areas. The strategy may address a perceived or hypothetical market that has not been tapped, and, though not responding directly to a customer's suggestion, it should nonetheless be based on awareness of customer need.

One obvious advantage of internally driven growth is that your company can focus exactly on what it does best, its core expertise, and design a product or service that fits your existing processes and business model. This can mean higher business efficiency, lower costs, and greater profits—*if* you can persuade a customer to buy. Because it's your idea, it's easier to plan and get moving on it, and you're probably more passionate about it as well.

The disadvantages of purely internal planning are equally obvious: a higher risk of failure and the high cost of developing the service and materials for selling your product or service "on the come." Even though you may have a strong relationship with your target customer, you're going in cold, hoping to fill a need the customer may not be fully aware of. And even though you may have done a careful analysis of your potential market, the fact that the idea comes from within may unconsciously prejudice your decision. Be careful not to fall in love with your own rosy expectations.

The fact that the idea comes from within may unconsciously prejudice your decision. Be careful not to fall in love with your own rosy expectations.

Although it's possible to achieve success either way, I recommend externally driven growth. It can lead your business into many new areas, new customer groups, new revenue streams, new geographic areas, even new industries. This is the way to get big—*fast*. It's the way I transformed my first marketing company from a $200,000-a-year business into a $30-million mini-Elephant in just five years. I accomplished this growth largely through identifying and addressing the needs of my customers and by virtue of my growing reputation for reliability and effectiveness. Later I leveraged my new business lines into megadeals with other organizations and $250 million annual sales.

So what's the downside? First, compared with internal growth planning, an external growth strategy requires a strong commitment from the sales force to dig into the customer's plans, processes, and bureaucracy. The sales force must already have a strong, trusting relationship with the customer, a relationship that may take years to establish and requires constant attention to maintain.

If you are the owner of the business, both you and your entire sales force must perfect the art of navigating the customer's bureaucracy. You need to know the system you are dealing with inside out—everything about the organization's structure, its processes, and its budget cycle:

- Whom do you approach?
- When?
- How?
- Who buys?
- Who influences buying decisions?
- Who makes the budget decisions?
- Who will go to bat for you?

It's not that externally driven development uniquely requires this level of customer knowledge; it's that your success virtually *depends* on it, whereas internally motivated growth presupposes less dependence.

> **Externally driven growth can lead your business into many new areas, new customer groups, new revenue streams, new geographic areas, even new industries.**

You and your sales force need to know the answers to these questions about the customer *before* the competition gets wind of them. This puts the burden of growth planning largely on the shoulders of your sales staff. For externally driven growth, you're using your eyes and ears—your salespeople—more than you're using the inner resources of imagination, projection, and analysis. That's why your salespeople need the extra motivation I talked about earlier.

As is the case in most businesses, those who succeed are those who are most flexible. The very best way to plan for growth is to be alert for what customers want or are planning to do, but also to keep everybody in your company thinking about how you can better market your current products or services and what you can sell in the future. At some point, a customer's expressed desire, or a latent need your salespeople have identified, will coincide with one of your new ideas, and that's what you can presell most readily. Stay alert for these opportunities.

Part IV

As Big as You Can Be

"When thinking about growth, many businesspeople equate 'complicated' with 'powerful.' This is a beginner's mistake."

How Do You Make
Your Money?

I n the last two sections I showed you how to assess the current health and solidity of your business, the potential and risks for growth, and the importance of the sales function in the development and success of your future growth strategies.

Those chapters set the stage for the thinking I'm going to ask you to do next. In this chapter and in the rest of part IV, I will walk you through a simple, systematic process to grow your business that involves evaluating how your business now operates; assessing the relative merits of horizontal and vertical growth, where your best opportunities lie, and the risk and potential of a given growth strategy; and learning how to keep track of the growth process and its results.

By following this procedure from chapter to chapter, you will lay the foundation for changes you can make that lead to substantial and sustainable growth.

So let's get going!

The first step is to ask yourself: How does my business make money?

The answer seems obvious, doesn't it? Your business makes money by selling specific goods or services to customers (for more money than it costs you to provide them, of course).

That's the short answer, but it doesn't really tell you much, does it? Selling goods or services to customers is how all businesses operate. To describe how your business in particular makes money, you have to be able to say exactly what it is that you are selling and exactly who it is that you are selling to.

Why is it important to know your current revenue streams and customers? Because the only way to explore the future effectively is to fully understand the present. Later you're going to explore new ways to make money and expand your customer base. By growing the what and/or the who, we're going to develop new growth strategies for your business.

The only way to explore the future effectively is to fully understand the present.

The What and the Who

To perform an in-depth analysis of how your business makes money, you need to identify in sufficient detail all the things you're doing that cause money to come to you. Not only that, you need to be able to describe in some detail your customers—the people or entities that buy your products or services. In short:

- What are your revenue streams?
- Who are your current target customers?

The first question is about where the money comes from. To arrive at a definitive answer, you have to identify every source of revenue. If you sell fifty different products, each of those is a *revenue source*. But that doesn't exhaust the possibilities. If, for example, you charge for shipping at breakeven, that's another revenue source. If you sell an extended warranty, that's yet another. (Remember, a product or service doesn't have to turn a profit to be a revenue source.) Even a small business can have a surprising number of revenue sources—many of which might represent untapped potential for growth.

As you will see, your revenue sources can be categorized for ease of analysis and planning. Groups of similar revenue sources form a *revenue stream*. You can think of revenue sources and revenue streams in terms of a supermarket: The individual products are the revenue sources, the categories listed on the overhead aisle signs are the revenue streams. To this basic structure you add other revenue streams such as shipping, packaging, or catering.

If you're operating a business with only a few product lines, you might identify as few as three to five revenue sources, and you might group these into one, two, or three revenue streams. But even a small business, such as a mom-and-pop hardware store, can have thousands of revenue sources (for example, hammers, saws, drills, screwdrivers, nails, staples, wood screws, metal screws, hinges, washers) that could be grouped into dozens of revenue streams (tools, building materials, lumber) or, at your discretion, boiled down to a basic few (hardware, packaging, shipping, contractor services). As you can see, the definition of categories is somewhat flexible. Identifying revenue sources, then grouping them into revenue streams, is part science and part art.

Identifying revenue sources, then grouping them into revenue streams, is part science and part art.

The second question delves into detail on the other side of the transaction. Who, exactly, is providing the money for your revenue sources? You need to know very specifically the kinds of customers you're dealing with now. This not only helps you shape new products and services to offer to them, but also lets you identify new and different customers for your current offerings or any new ideas you come up with.

The Lineup

To illustrate how revenue sources and revenue streams are identified, I will use several real-life business examples (with names and revealing details disguised) from four industries:

Roy's BBQ. This barbecue joint is run by Theo Washington and his family. Known for its terrific sauces, Roy's is a favorite among Chicago's many barbecue restaurants. Its food sales exceeded $200,000 last year.

Abel Box Company. Owned by Larry Abel, this Florida-based company is a broker for corrugated boxes. Abel doesn't manufacture the boxes, but it represents several manufacturers and sells boxes to customers. Since it has close relationships with a number of suppliers, Abel can shop around for low prices and fast delivery. Abel hit $500,000 in sales last year.

You've Got It Maid. This home-based cleaning service in the nation's capital is owned by Olga Helenovich. Olga and her crew of five clean dozens of homes in four affluent suburban neighborhoods. Olga's company cleared $150,000 in profits last year.

Sure Shot Collectibles. Peter Martsmann's San Francisco-based company provides an online auction where customers can buy art and sports collectibles. Like the better-known eBay, Sure Shot doesn't own the products but rather facilitates deals between buyers and sellers. Peter's business generated more than $25 million in sales last year.

Follow along as we browse through these business examples over the next several chapters. Each one has key

Company	Industry	Product
Roy's BBQ	Restaurant	Sandwiches, ribs, chicken, BBQ sauce
Abel Box Company	Broker	Corrugated boxes, dividers
You've Got It Maid	Maid service	Home cleaning
Sure Shot Collectibles	Internet marketplace	Online service for consumers to bid on art & sports collectibles

characteristics that can help you see the finer points of this analysis. Once you've gained an understanding of each step of the process, walk through it with your own company in mind, applying the concepts to your own business operation. This will help you organize your information and ideas as you formulate the most effective growth strategy for your business.

Revenue Streams and Their Sources

The first thing you need is a clear and exact understanding of how your business makes its money. What we're looking for here isn't simply a listing of products or services. Yes, we want those, but that's only the beginning. We'll start by identifying your revenue sources, then we'll group these into specific categories, or revenue streams.

Some of you might already be structuring your business by revenue streams. If you are, you have a head start, but stick around—you've still got to go through this step, because the smart money says you'll identify one or more additional streams that you haven't thought of before.

In order to derive your revenue streams, you'll need input from your sales force, operations personnel, and accounting department. Don't overlook your billing invoices or other sources of information that others may not be aware of.

1. List your sources of revenue. Write down every way that you take in money, whether from sales or other sources. Don't think in terms of profit; although your main revenue sources, from which you derive a profit, may be obvious, be sure to include every possible way your company brings in money. It's easy to overlook certain revenue sources that are operational in nature and don't generate profit, such as shipping charges that were paid separately or charged at cost. One way to discover these sources is to carefully review all invoices and account for every dollar taken into the business over the past year.

Now for our sample companies. Roy's BBQ makes most of its money selling food selections off its menu, but the company also peddles its world-class sauce to its customers. Similarly, Abel Box Company makes 95 percent of its sales from boxes and dividers, but also charges some customers a warehouse fee if they buy a large order for piecemeal delivery. Both Roy's sauce and Abel's warehouse fee would be listed as sources of revenue (and, as you will see, separate revenue streams).

2. Analyze your revenue sources. Take a hard look at each revenue source on your list and write yourself a short note of explanation for each. Here's what Abel Box Company would write down:

Company	Revenue Sources	Notes
Abel Box Company	4 x 4 x 4 boxes	Standard size box
	8 x 8 x 8 boxes	Standard size box
	#8 partitions	Standard partition
	#10 partitions	Standard partition
	Graphics	Design fee (at cost)
	Film work	Design fee (at cost)
	Plates	Design fee (at cost)
	Shipping	To customer (at cost)
	Storage	Inventory storage (at cost)

3. Group revenue sources into revenue streams. Based on your notes for each source, categorize similar revenue sources into revenue streams. Give each revenue stream a descriptive name (for example, the first four revenue sources above can be placed in the group "Standard corrugated boxes and partitions"). These are examples of the types of ways a business makes its money.

The chart on the facing page lists products and revenue streams for each of our four companies. Note the different ways the companies categorize their revenue streams. Roy, for example, can now look at his business more strategically by dividing the whole into parts: base menu and sauce sales.

Customers and Their Attributes

Now that you've identified your revenue streams, your next step is to identify the "who"—that is, who your current

Company	Products/Services	Revenue Streams
Roy's BBQ	Sandwiches, ribs, chicken & barbecue sauce	Base menu items Sauce sales (minimal)
Abel Box Company	Corrugated boxes & dividers	Standard corrugated boxes & partitions Design fees for box Fees for shipping to customer Fees for storing inventory
You've Got It Maid	Home cleaning Floor & window cleaning	Weekly home cleanings Specialized cleaning
Sure Shot Collectibles	Online service for consumers to bid on art & sports collectibles	Service charge per order or item Fee for posting on the web Ad design & copy fee Special features spot fee

customers are. In order to expand on your customer base effectively, you must first define it accurately.

1. Define a customer base for each revenue stream. Be specific. Defining your target audience as families is not enough; you need to know that it's families with two working parents and an income exceeding $50,000, living within ten miles of your store.

Some of your revenue streams may have several target customers. One of the businesses of which I'm part owner is eSkape, a 60,000-square-foot family entertainment center. eSkape has 38 bowling lanes, a restaurant, bar, game room, party rooms, laser tag, grill, and more. As you can see, I've already named seven revenue streams, but the customer breakdown is far more complex. Each revenue stream has several customer bases, and many of these target markets vary by time of day and season. For example, the restaurant targets businesspeople for its weekly lunch fare, families for dinner and weekends, and young adults for late-night pit stops. The bowling revenue stream targets leagues during the day and during soft spots in the schedule, but targets

Company	Revenue Stream	Current Target Customer
Roy's BBQ	*Base Menu Items*	
	Lunch	Office workers in groups of 2–4, employed primarily by companies within a 5-mile radius of the store
		Local high school students
	Dinner	Families with children living or working within 10 miles of the store
		Young adults & couples aged 18–25 with incomes under $30,000
	Pickup window	Mothers picking up dinner for the family within a 15-mile radius of their home
		Singles aged 18–25 commuting from work
	Sauce	Frequent customers (to date, only a few sales)
Abel Box Company	Standard boxes & partitions	Box buyers in manufacturing & retail sectors
		Primarily Florida companies that typically require more than 50,000 boxes per year
	Design fees	Smaller companies lacking art departments
		Large companies that don't want to risk in-house delays
		Clients who have sent in their design incorrectly & require corrections
	Freight	Companies lacking shipping departments or a desire to set up one
		Companies that order large quantities & ask for staggered shipments
	Storage fees	Companies unable to accept shipment after ordering goods
		Companies prone to modifying their orders

Company	Revenue Stream	Current Target Customer
You've Got It Maid	Home cleaning, floor & window cleaning	Upscale homeowners in four neighborhoods Families with children; income $100,000+ Half have two adults working, half have one adult working
Sure Shot Collectibles	Service charge per order (buyer)	Online users & collectors Incomes $90,000+ College graduates or postgrads Aged 40–60 Mostly experienced online buyers
	Posting fee to site (seller)	Half are first-time sellers
	Ad design & copy fee	Income $40,000–$75,000
	Special features spot fee	70% aged 30–40 15% aged 20–29 15% aged 41+

individuals as its customer base for open play on nights and weekends; and this changes a bit in the summer months, when the target is children from day camps.

2. Consider each revenue stream individually. Consult as many sources as you can to sharpen your focus: marketing staff, salespeople, friends, family, advertising agencies, your customer database, industry data, and more. Of course, to get hands-on data, you'll also want to monitor your customers as they purchase your products or services. Define each customer base in as much detail as possible, and remember that the more you know about your current customers, the more effective you'll be in developing growth strategies. For each revenue stream, try to determine the following information about your customers. Much of this data can be

Getting Information

Regardless of the industry you're in, you can conduct your own research to get customer information. Ideally, you'd get the scoop directly from your customers by charting who is considering your product and then monitoring their purchasing habits. This is easy in industries such as retail, where you're face-to-face with customers every day. If you can't get information directly from the customer, enlist your salespeople or customer service in the effort. Develop a questionnaire (use the same one for both groups) and have them fill one out for each customer they handle. Then review the results with them and also compare how each department filled out the questionnaires. The different results may surprise you, but the answers will tell you a lot and help you refine your research methods. If you have an online business, you can set it up to record the metrics automatically: number of visits, navigation through your site, time on site, detailed demographic data, and so forth.

grouped into ranges, which should be kept as tight as possible to provide more accurate and detailed information.

Demographics. What statistics can you attribute to your current customers? Include the following categories:

- Age
- Sex
- Income
- Marital status
- Education

Psychographics. Knowing lifestyle characteristics will help sharpen your picture of your customers. Examples might include people who eat dinner out two or more times per week, visit health clubs, take two vacations per year, follow new fashions, have kids who attend overnight summer camp, buy online, or collect antiques. You can often get this information directly from your customers by using a brief questionnaire (keep it short) or focused conversation.

Geography. Where do your customers live? If your business draws local customers, map out the radius around your company that you believe captures your base.

Miscellaneous. List any additional information you believe might help you home in on your current target customers. For example, Sure Shot could ask for its customers' favorite websites if they felt that the information would be helpful in understanding their customers.

Once you've analyzed how you make your money and who you make it from, it's time to move on and determine the best growth strategy to follow.

Horizontal and Vertical Growth

By this time, you've identified all the ways your company makes money, and you've focused your attention on understanding the DNA of your current customers. Believe it or not, you now know more about your own business than most business owners do about theirs.

Now what you need is a powerful strategy for growing your business—along with a blueprint for expanding your business platform to facilitate the large increases in sales and profits that you expect.

When thinking about growth, many businesspeople equate "complicated" with "powerful." This is a beginner's mistake. Over the years, I've heard, seen, and studied many plans for growth, and the best plans are usually the simplest ones. Complexity in planning is often unnecessary, sometimes even counterproductive.

In my direct experience—which includes tons of business growth and, yes, a few disasters as well—there are two, and only two, possible growth strategies:

1. Vertical growth. Focusing on your current customers and getting them to buy new products or services.

2. Horizontal growth. Finding new customers to buy existing products or services.

This chapter is about the fundamentals of these strategies. The rest of the chapters in this section will guide you through the process of figuring out which strategy is best for you and your business. Follow the steps and develop lists for both vertical and horizontal opportunities. Consult other people, both inside and outside your business. Don't be afraid of ideas that seem far-fetched or out of reach. If there ever was a time for brainstorming, this is it.

> **The best plans are usually the simplest ones.**

Upward and Outward

Josefina Manauta owns Descubrir, Inc., a small but successful two-person business in Chicago. Descubrir (which is Spanish for "discover") translates training materials from English to Spanish for businesses needing to communicate important issues, such as safety, to their Spanish-speaking employees. The business was doing well but got most of its revenues from just one large customer. Josefina knew that she had to reduce her client dependency by expanding her customer base. But that was another issue; for now, the concern was how best to grow her business. She had been trying to get more customers for her translation service, but the demands of the existing large customer didn't leave her with much time to prospect.

The good thing was that her company had a great relationship with her big customer that perhaps could be leveraged for growth opportunities. In fact, she had recently signed a multiple-year contract with this customer to supply the same translation services.

Josefina figured that her best and only practical option for growth would be to sell more and different items to her current big customer. She set out to capitalize on her relationships and her access to different people within that organization, in order to determine what other products or services Descubrir might provide.

A few days later, Josefina was meeting with her customer, reviewing the latest materials to be translated, just as she had done many times before. But on this day she was focused on growing her business. She asked her contact just one question: "How are you using the materials my company translates?" The answer: "We hand them out during in-house training classes for our employees." Out of this brief exchange was born a new and successful service.

The idea was simple. The new service Descubrir would now offer its large customer would extend beyond the translation of training materials: Descubrir's people would conduct the training classes themselves. Juanita reasoned that (1) one of her company's available skill resources— Spanish-speaking employees—was not being fully utilized, (2) her company could do the training cheaper than her customer's own organization could, and (3) the customer would jump at the chance to cut costs and simplify things by outsourcing the entire training process. It was that easy.

Vertical Growth Strategy

With a vertical growth strategy you find new products and services that appeal to the customers you already have. The following tactics will help you identify new offerings for your business:

1. Sell more of the same products or services to your existing customers. Consider hiring more salespeople or changing your sales policy or commission structure to motivate your sales team.

2. Extend your line to offer current customers a new product or service that either complements or upgrades a product or service you've already been offering.

3. Develop entirely new products or services to appeal to your existing customers' demographic and psychographic profiles.

In short order, Josefina developed a business model around her new service to ensure that she was set up for success (see part II, On Solid Ground, for details on how to develop your business model). Then she called her contact in the company. He loved the idea. He set up a meeting for her to present the new opportunity. Josefina walked away with a

Horizontal Growth Strategy

With a horizontal growth strategy, you seek out new customers to whom you can sell either existing products and services or new ones. Bear in mind, however, that you need to be ready to modify your product line to suit your new target customers' needs.

Two main options are available:

1. Expand the geographic reach of your business, but sell the same product. In other words, you're looking for the same sort of people, but in a new neighborhood, state, or region.

2. Sell to different types of customers in the same geographical area.

sale on the spot—but, more important, Descubrir had now created a bigger business platform (framework for future growth).

A year later, this new service had not only become the largest part of Josefina's business, it was the catalyst for 300 percent growth in less than one year, to sales of over $1 million. She hired more employees and—changing growth direction from vertical to horizontal—began selling her services to another company, thus reducing her client dependency as well. Not bad for a two-person start-up.

Broader Horizons

Don and Barbara Simms own Berry Best, a company that makes great gourmet strawberry treats with many flavors of coatings and toppings (including my favorite, Berry Chocolate). Berry Best sold its strawberries to individuals online and by direct mail. Sales were okay, but Don and Barbara knew they needed to grow to survive, and competition was tough.

They thought about a vertical strategy, expanding their product line to include gourmet apples and shortbread, but they didn't have the equipment, money, or expertise necessary to add to their flagship offering. So they set out to grow by selling their gourmet strawberries to a whole new audience. This would also require investment, but not nearly as much as it would for adding new products. They could handle it without going deep into debt.

After much study and discussion, they set their sights on two new but related customer groups: catering companies and party planners. This growth strategy would require them to sell their candied strawberries in bulk quantities, which meant that new pricing and packaging would also be needed.

In less than six months, Don and Barbara were up to their necks in orders. Caterers loved the berries; they were a unique and popular new delicacy for their clients, and the price was low enough to offer a unique item at a competitive price while still making good money with a traditional markup.

The Best of Both Worlds

I know what you're thinking: Is this strictly an either-or proposition? The answer is no—you don't have to limit yourself to just a vertical or horizontal growth strategy. You can use both strategies in combination. That's the way to take full advantage of all your opportunities for growth, and to develop a business platform that can yield heavy growth in the future by selling more products and services to more and more groups of customers. Often, one path leads naturally to the other—expanding your line of products and services provides a platform for reaching new customers, and vice versa.

You don't have to limit yourself to just a vertical or horizontal growth strategy. You can use both strategies in combination.

In actuality, if you're a small- or medium-sized business aspiring to Elephanthood, it's rare that you would use both vertical and horizontal growth strategies simultaneously. Your resources for growth—cash, equipment, personnel, and focus—would probably be limited. Since you aren't yet the Elephant you aspire to be, you'll need to take on as little risk as possible while you grow.

If you're a translation service operating under a multiyear contract with one big client, a staff of yourself plus one, and a few pieces of office equipment, you may see the need to sell your services to many more customers in order to ensure the long-range survival of your business. But the market for your particular service niche is limited, and so the quickest (and safest) strategy is to maximize your potential by offering new services to your existing large customer. This is what Josefina Manauta did.

If you're a small manufacturer of gourmet foods, offering a few, specialized, high-end strawberry confections directly to a broad, shallow market of end consumers, you may foresee the profits to be made from expanding your range of products to those customers. But first, to invest in the expensive new equipment you will need if you wish to offer these new products, you'll have to sell a lot more of your existing product. That means finding more customers—and that is what Don and Barbara Simms did.

So, if you're Josefina, let's say that your vertical growth strategy is working. By offering your new bilingual training service, you've created new streams of revenue and generated enough cash flow to rent a larger office, hire new employees, and invest in new equipment. You're doing a good job and getting recognition for it, and you're reaping the financial gain from the growth. This could be your signal to begin looking into a horizontal growth mode. Who knows, your grateful customer might even refer your services to other companies that don't compete with it.

Small or large, you shouldn't try to do everything at once; concentrate on one strategy at a time.

Look what you've got going for you. Instead of occupying a narrow service niche of merely translating documents, you're offering a range of services (translation, training, Spanish-language classes) that makes you more attractive to a broader base of customers. By growing vertically at first, you've increased the value of your offerings in a way that has not only brought you new business from an old customer but made it possible for you to grow horizontally by attracting new customers—which Josefina has begun to do.

Don and Barbara could approach a combination strategy from the other direction—horizontal first. By expanding their customer base, they raise new revenues that could potentially be invested in new equipment, which would allow

The Companies (Continued)

The previous chapter identified the revenue streams for our four example businesses (restaurant, corrugated box manufacturer, maid service, and online auction). Here we'll build on that by adding potential growth strategies. The purpose is to clarify the difference between vertical and horizontal growth. Try to think of other strategies, both vertical and horizontal, for each of the examples.

Company	Revenue Stream	Vertical Growth	Horizontal Growth
Abel Box	Standard boxes	Sell packing supplies Sell custom boxes	Sell to smaller companies and new industries, perhaps selling specialized boxes to ad agencies Expand beyond Florida
Roy's BBQ	Dinner	Add beer & wine to menu Add delivery service	Create a brand of sauce for retail sales Open second store Franchise the business
You've Got It Maid	Cleaning service	Add drapery & carpet shampoo Add window cleaning Provide hostess service for dinner parties	Expand services beyond the current four neighborhoods Focus on new customers in four neighborhoods, perhaps singles or neighbors of current customers
Sure Shot Collectibles	Service charge per order (buyer)	Offer new products for bidding (beyond art & sports collectibles)	Expand customer base through links with other Internet marketplaces

them to expand their range of product offerings. They would also have the advantage of developing sound relationships with more customers, a critical component in the success of future product offerings. The ensuing vertical growth would be in the form of expanding sales of new products to existing customers. Persuading old customers to do new kinds of business with you is relatively easy, because they know you and (presumably) trust you.

Small or large, you shouldn't try to do everything at once; concentrate on one strategy at a time. If you're already well on your way to becoming an Elephant, it's not so hard to rub your stomach and pat your head simultaneously. But you've still got to watch where you're walking. Even the big ones trip up sometimes.

The Growth Matrix

Y ou've identified your revenue sources and grouped them into revenue streams; you've sharpened your picture of your customer base for each revenue stream; you've identified some candidates for vertical and horizontal growth strategies. Now you're going to assemble all this information to help you decide on the best growth strategy for your business. I like to call this array Kaplan's Growth Matrix, but for convenience we'll just refer to it here as "the matrix."

We'll use the matrix to organize your information in such a way that you will see white space in areas you are not serving with products, services, or customers. This white space represents opportunities for growth.

The Template

The first step is to set up a template. Since your business is probably different from any of the ones I'm using as examples, you'll need to construct your own template, using mine as a general guide.

You can draw up a matrix template by (1) drawing horizontal and vertical lines on blank paper or printing grid paper that you've downloaded (Google "grid paper"), or by (2) using a spreadsheet program or other graphing software to set up the template on your computer screen. You'll need more than one template, because you're going to draw a matrix for each revenue stream.

Each matrix has a horizontal axis and a vertical axis. Across the top of the matrix for your first revenue stream, list the target customer groups you've identified for that revenue stream. These will represent opportunities for horizontal growth. Down the left side, list your products and services that make up this revenue stream. These will reveal opportunities for vertical growth.

If your target customers can be defined in different ways, use a separate matrix for each one. Abel Box Company's standard boxes and partitions, for example, would use three matrices: target industries, target geography, and target client size.

ABEL BOX COMPANY Revenue Stream: Standard Boxes & Partitions—Industry		
REVENUE SOURCE	MANUFACTURING	RETAIL STORES
Standard boxes 4 x 4 x 4		
Standard boxes 8 x 8 x 8		
Standard partitions #8		
Standard partitions #10		

ABEL BOX COMPANY Revenue Stream: Standard Boxes & Partitions—Geography		
REVENUE SOURCE	DADE COUNTY, FLORIDA	BROWARD COUNTY, FLORIDA
Standard boxes 4 x 4 x 4		
Standard boxes 8 x 8 x 8		
Standard partitions #8		
Standard partitions #10		

ABEL BOX COMPANY Revenue Stream: Standard Boxes & Partitions—Client Size		
REVENUE SOURCE	LARGE	MEDIUM
Standard boxes 4 x 4 x 4		
Standard boxes 8 x 8 x 8		
Standard partitions #8		
Standard partitions #10		

Customers

The next step is to identify the target customers for each product or service, in all of the different ways you've grouped your customers. In each matrix, mark an X to indicate that you are currently selling a given product or service to a given customer in a given geographic area. In the example shown here, Abel sells standard $8 \times 8 \times 8$ boxes to retail stores but not to manufacturers, in both Dade County and Broward County, and to large clients but not medium-size ones.

ABEL BOX COMPANY
Revenue Stream: Standard Boxes & Partitions—Industry

REVENUE SOURCE	MANUFACTURING	RETAIL STORES
Standard boxes 4 x 4 x 4	X	X
Standard boxes 8 x 8 x 8		X
Standard partitions #8	X	
Standard partitions #10	X	X

ABEL BOX COMPANY
Revenue Stream: Standard Boxes & Partitions—Geography

REVENUE SOURCE	DADE COUNTY, FLORIDA	BROWARD COUNTY, FLORIDA
Standard boxes 4 x 4 x 4	X	X
Standard boxes 8 x 8 x 8	X	X
Standard partitions #8	X	X
Standard partitions #10	X	X

ABEL BOX COMPANY
Revenue Stream: Standard Boxes & Partitions—Client Size

REVENUE SOURCE	LARGE	MEDIUM
Standard boxes 4 x 4 x 4	X	X
Standard boxes 8 x 8 x 8	X	
Standard partitions #8	X	
Standard partitions #10	X	X

Growth Opportunities

Here's where things start to come together. It's time now to zero in on that next big growth idea. Should you squeeze more products into your customers, more customers out of your products, or both? Let's get to work!

Look at each revenue stream, one matrix at a time. Extend the horizontal axis, and at the top of the new columns this opens up, write down as many new kinds of customers (industry type, geographic area, size) as you can think of who might buy your current products or services. Be creative; be imaginative; be expansive. The more ideas, the better. (This is where you really need input from your employees—sales, support, management—for those blind spots in your own thinking.) We'll sift through these possibilities later to sort out the best ones.

In our Abel Box example, as you can see in the next set of tables, we've come up with new target customers (indicated in **boldface**) for one revenue stream in three categories— industry, geography, and company size. Keep in mind that Abel has other revenue streams that can be explored for horizontal growth potential: design fees, shipping fees, and storage fees. Here we will focus our attention on one revenue stream only: standard boxes and partitions.

In how many directions can you grow?

Once the horizontal axis is complete, move on to the vertical axis. Add as many new products (or services) as possible for both your current and potential customers (indicated in the horizontal axis). As before, make sure to heavily involve your sales force here; they know best what customers need. Take your time, be creative, and consult with experts inside and outside your company. Remember to consider what your competitors are doing as well. (Like the new customers, the new product opportunities for Abel are shown here in bold type.)

Abel Box Company has white spaces—let's call them opportunities—at the following junctures on the first matrix: opportunities for new industries (on the horizontal

ABEL BOX COMPANY
Revenue Stream: Standard Boxes & Partitions by Industry

REVENUE SOURCE	MANUFACTURING	RETAIL STORES	MOVING COMPANIES	CO-PACKERS	AD AGENCIES
Standard boxes 4 x 4 x 4	X	X			
Standard boxes 8 x 8 x 8		X			
Standard partitions #8	X				
Standard partitions #10	X	X			
Custom boxes					
Custom partitions					
Packing tape					
Bubble packing					
Foam peanuts					

ABEL BOX COMPANY
Revenue Stream: Standard Boxes & Partitions by Geography

REVENUE SOURCE	MIAMI, FLORIDA	ORLANDO, FLORIDA	JACKSONVILLE, FLORIDA	ATLANTA, GEORGIA	SAVANNAH, GEORGIA
Standard boxes 4 x 4 x 4	X	X			
Standard boxes 8 x 8 x 8	X	X			
Standard partitions #8	X	X			
Standard partitions #10	X	X			
Custom boxes					
Custom partitions					
Packing tape					
Bubble packing					
Foam peanuts					

ABEL BOX COMPANY
Revenue Stream: Standard Boxes & Partitions by Client Size

REVENUE SOURCE	LARGE	MEDIUM	SMALL
Standard boxes 4 x 4 x 4	X	X	
Standard boxes 8 x 8 x 8		X	
Standard partitions #8	X		
Standard partitions #10	X	X	
Custom boxes			
Custom partitions			
Packing tape			
Bubble packing			
Foam peanuts			

axis), including moving companies, co-packers, and ad agencies, for all products (new and existing); opportunities for existing customers in manufacturing and retail stores (with two existing products) and all the new products (on the vertical axis).

After you complete this step, you will have compiled all the necessary information for each revenue stream including current target customers, potential new customers, current products, and potential new products. Any square on any matrix that doesn't have an X in it represents a potential growth strategy—and thus a potential pot of gold.

Operational Mandates

Now I'll show you a way to add growth strategies that come as close as you'll get to a sure thing. They are called operational mandates, and after you read this section you should be eager to identify those in your own business.

I can't even tell you how many businesses I've been able to grow by simply expanding or adding a revenue stream to include an operational mandate. The beauty of this is that often it's easy to get customers to prebuy this service or product because they are already using it indirectly. Customers who are buying Abel's corrugated boxes receive them from Abel, so they are probably already using Abel as a shipper, even though the costs are baked into the price. It's less of a leap to persuade a customer to use Abel's shipping services for shipping something else—because the customer is already having a good shipping experience with Abel.

Turning something that costs you money on the operational side of the business into something that makes you money on the revenue side— what a beautiful thing! Not only does making this change provide greater cash flow and profits from the new revenue, it often results in a higher margin for your core business.

How do you identify an operational mandate? It's not difficult. You simply chart the things your business does to execute contracts with your customers. Follow an order or contract through your business—from the actions you take to obtain products or services to sell, all the way to delivery or pickup by the customer. Operational mandates typically are actions you've performed so many times that you don't even think about them, but that have become areas of expertise.

Create a flowchart, a timeline, or even a simple list. Be thorough; don't overlook the smallest tasks. Each step in your process, even a seemingly insignificant one, has

New from Old

The fact is, many successful new business growth initiatives stem from current business. When you're successful at growing your business, the products and services you sell will be different a year down the road. Converting operational cost centers into revenue streams just might be the most important piece of business growth advice I could pass on to you.

Here's an added benefit: Plotting your operational processes will provide you a unique opportunity to gauge your operational efficiencies. Take note as you walk through the operational steps in your business to see if, in fact, you are running efficiently.

the potential to become a revenue stream—or at least a new product or service (vertical axis) for the target markets you've identified (horizontal axis).

As an example, let's say you have a business that delivers a product—pizzas to households or corrugated boxes to other businesses, it really doesn't matter what. After delivering these products for a while, your company will have developed a certain degree of expertise in delivery. Who's to say that couldn't be a new revenue stream for the business?

Core Business: the things your business does best. Answer this question: "What does your business do?"

Operational Mandates: the things you must do to execute on your contracts, including obtaining the products and services to sell.

Mandate for Success

One of my businesses was a marketing company that specialized in distributing materials such as coupons and product samples on behalf of customers (mostly packaged goods companies) to specific target markets—new mothers, kids 6–12, teens—through venues such as hospitals and schools. We billed our customers based on the number of product samples or coupons we delivered to the target market.

As was common in the industry, many of our customers would do market research to gauge the effectiveness of our marketing programs. Based on the results, they would give us more business, less business, or no further business. As part of the preparation phase, a client would require us to prepare lists of consumers who would be getting the coupons or samples. The client would prepare a similar list of consumers, with the same demographic profile, who would not get the materials. These *prelists* were given to an independent market research firm, which contacted the consumers on both lists and measured the difference in purchasing levels between the two.

Our customers' market research people actually hated developing these prelists because it took so long. Since research was so important to our clients, and because we knew they hated it, and because we were already spending a lot of time and money on our part of it, we decided to look at it as a growth opportunity.

Turning something that costs you money on the operational side of the business into something that makes you money on the revenue side— what a beautiful thing!

We approached the market research department at one of our large clients and offered to relieve them of their market research headaches. We would take over all the preparation by developing both lists and getting them to the independent firm for implementation. We would send an employee to them for training and would do the work exactly the way they wanted it done. Our fee would be less than the expense of doing it internally.

About a year later, we were billing $1.5 million, more than a third of it profit. Three years into it, this new service of ours was generating over $8 million in sales and $2.5 million in profit. Not bad, right? The key to this new service was the fact that we had already been performing in the market research arena, albeit as a cost component and in a support role. The research expertise we had developed over the years enabled us to take this cost component and turn it into a big-time revenue stream with a high profit margin—all this from an operational mandate, something we had to do to deliver on our contracts.

If you look at your business, you'll probably find operational mandates that have the potential to become profitable revenue streams. List as many as you can think of. Keep your list with the other information you've developed to date. Don't worry—we won't leave it alone for long.

Risk vs. Reward

Now that you've opened up all that white space and discovered a wealth of opportunities in your business, it's time to see which ones will give you your best shot at successful growth. You'll see right away that some of them are intrinsically riskier or less practical than others; you can put these aside and concentrate on the five or so that you think have the greatest promise. In this chapter, we'll conduct a ten-step analysis to rank the opportunities in terms of their probability of success. Then you'll know which ones to chase and which to erase.

I evaluate each growth opportunity by comparing its potential risk with its possible rewards. I learned quite a while back that growth for the sake of growth is meaningless; I also learned that some ways to grow don't entail much risk. Since that time, balancing risks against rewards has served me well. I've even invented a risk assessment worksheet that guides you through the task, as you will see later in the chapter.

Rewards

We'll deal with the positives first. Look at all the white spaces and list the growth opportunities they represent. For each potential growth

> **Unless you're doing it to solve a cash flow problem, getting more revenue and more employees without profits is a recipe for headaches and disaster.**

option, consider the upside: finances, reputation, organization, long-term impact, and any other positives you can think of that might come as a result of this new business effort. Ask yourself the following questions:

Financial rewards. Will the opportunity make money? This is the most important question. If the answer is no, you've got two options: either (1) adjust your business model so that it will make money, or (2) toss the opportunity out the window.

Go beyond the obvious here. Will adding this new target customer or new product or service increase your bottom line, or just your sales? Unless you're doing it to solve a cash flow problem, getting more revenue and more employees without profits is a recipe for headaches and disaster. Or will the costs of generating the new product or service be absorbed by your current business, thereby yielding a higher profit margin in the long run?

Suppose you're thinking of expanding into another locale. How much will this increase your sales? How much more will it cost? Will you need a larger sales force? More staff to process orders? More office space? Will inventory or manufacturing costs rise? In estimating profits and costs and in building your business model, look ahead at least three to five years.

Reputation rewards. Will the growth opportunity give you more credibility in the marketplace? With current customers? With employees?

Organizational rewards. How would this opportunity affect company culture? Would it help you streamline your day-to-day operations? Boost morale? Get more bang for the buck from your current employees and operations?

Long-term rewards. Would it give you a foothold for a future opportunity? See if your idea moves you closer to your long-term vision. For example, if you have long-terms plans to expand your company from selling locally to selling nationally, determine whether the new opportunity would move you closer to that goal.

Risks

After considering the upside of each growth opportunity, carefully pull your head out of the clouds and realistically examine the difficulties and risks. If the problems you uncover seem excessive, scratch that opportunity and move on to the next. In most cases, if you do an objective analysis and keep your business and personal objectives in mind, you can avoid the fatal mistakes that many businesses make. I repeat: Some of the best decisions you'll make are the things you decide *not* to do.

Financial risk. Do the potential financial gains and other possible advantages justify the money and effort needed to implement the opportunity? Work out in detail what it will cost you to maximize each remaining growth opportunity, including the cost of goods sold, personnel, and space, as well as opportunity costs to your present business—that is, foreclosure of other opportunities.

Reputation risk. Could this strategy harm your reputation? Would geographical expansion damage your home-town image? Would a bigger operation slow your delivery time when speed of service is your prime selling point? Will your growth make current customers feel you're neglecting them? And don't forget to consider the impact of controversial new products—like the convenience store that lost a lot of family business when it began carrying adult-only magazines.

Organizational risk. Can you develop the opportunity without getting distracted from your current business? Will you need to change your day-to-day operations? Do you have the personnel to implement this idea? If not, can you hire them easily? Will you need to hire, fire, or reclassify employees? How will that affect morale?

Long-term risk. Will the opportunity pull your business away from your long-term vision for it? Does it rely on elements or conditions that may be transient—a fad, an election, seasonality? Are you at risk from a shift in government policy that might leave your business high and dry, but still burdened with the extra expenses?

When Smaller Is Bigger

Tammi Nuania is the owner and creative influence behind Enzio's Pizzeria, a family business with a homey feel that specializes in the kind of thick, deep-dish Chicago-style pizza that people line up around the corner to eat. Business was so good that it was common for customers to wait up to an hour for a table. Enzio's was bringing in $600,000 a year in sales and netting just over $200,000 before taxes—a tidy profit, because Tammi and her son, the chef, were taking generous salaries as well.

Tammi wanted Enzio's to grow and serve more people. She considered two options: (1) leasing a newer, larger, nicer building in the same neighborhood, or (2) a modest expansion into the space next door. She really liked the idea of the new, larger restaurant. It would be about four times the size of her original, quaint but successful pizzeria and would have a state-of-the-art kitchen, electronic registers—the whole bit. Enzio's would be going Hollywood.

But before Tammi inked the lease paperwork, she agreed to take a detailed look at how this strategy would impact her financials. This turned out to be a wise move.

The numbers showed that after about a year of transition and construction the business would be cooking again and that Enzio's would be packed. Tammi projected that sales would soar to $1,200,000—huge for her industry and a success by most standards. Then she looked at the profit projections—and almost keeled over. The new technology, space, staff, and operating costs would overwhelm the business. Although projected sales would double to $1,200,000, the pretax profit would still be the same, around $200,000. This meant that her profit margin (total profit divided by total sales) would fall from 33 percent in the old Enzio's

Other risks. For more details concerning risk, review the discussion in part II, chapter 6 on assessing risk in the business model.

History shows that successful growth initiatives are most likely to be those that draw on your area of expertise, let you rely on your current employees without hiring too many additional people, and can be sold to your current customers.

to 17 percent in the new—a disaster, should she ever decide to sell her business.

Tammi couldn't believe it—but the numbers didn't lie. So what would this huge expansion bring her, aside from the prestige of having a nicer-looking place? Nothing but aggravation. Her workload would increase. Her operating processes would change. Expenses would soar, because the new equipment would have to run even during slow periods. Risks and stress would grow—but not the bottom line.

She revisited the other growth option: a modest expansion into the vacant space next door. After running the numbers, she was amazed. By utilizing the additional space, expanding and improving the existing kitchen, and adding more tables, she could shift her business into overdrive. Projected sales were $900,000, but profits would now be $350,000, boosting her profit margin to nearly 40 percent. There were other benefits, too:

- The increase in sales and profits would kick in much sooner.

- The business would increase its profit margin through economies of scale.

- Staying in the same location would save time, effort, and the cost of redirecting customers.

- The family ambience, a major selling point, could be preserved.

- If sales dipped a bit, the monthly nut wouldn't cripple the business, so the risk was much lower.

Needless to say, this decision was a no-brainer, and Enzio's is now selling more deep-dish pies than ever.

Growth Opportunity Rankings

By this time, you've sifted through many growth opportunities, identified several that are financially promising and not too risky, and tossed the obvious clunkers. Now it's time to ask and answer your central question: Which of the remaining growth opportunities is the best one for you?

What follows is the key to getting that answer: my Growth Opportunity Rankings (GOR). Based on 15-plus years of my own experience, coupled with analysis by finance experts and researchers, the GOR systematically ranks growth opportunities, using appropriate criteria, and shows you which ones have the best chance for success and which ones should be put on hold or written off.

The GOR asks you to rank each surviving opportunity in ten key areas that are critical for new business success. Then you assign point values to each ranking in each category and tally up the scores to determine your best options. Here's how:

1. Photocopy the tally worksheet below, or download the form from the website **www.differencemaker.com** (go to "Freebies") and print it out.

2. Select your top five growth opportunities (or fewer, if you prefer). Name them Opportunity A, Opportunity B, and so forth, in no particular order, or assign code names so you can remember which is which.

3. Enter the opportunities on the form, ranked from best to worst, in each of the following categories (note that some categories are assigned higher point values due to their greater impact on success):

- **Current customers.** How much does the opportunity enable you to sell to the same customers as your current core business does?
- **Financial impact.** How big is the financial upside for the opportunity? (Include factors such as those having the biggest home run potential and those that most increase your overall profit margin.)
- **Organizational impact.** To what extent does the opportunity allow you to keep your current organization intact without having to hire a lot of new employees?
- **Leadership.** Is someone available to lead the effort if you adopt this opportunity?
- **Similar industry or business.** Does the opportunity target the same industry as your current business does, or at least a complementary industry from an operational mandate?

Growth Opportunity Ranking Worksheet

Rank each of the opportunities from the best to the worst in each of the following categories.

Current Customers	Financial Impact	Organizational Impact	Leadership
Points	Points	Points	Points
(22)	(18)	(12)	(13)
(20)	(14)	(8)	(8)
(10)	(8)	(6)	(6)
(4)	(4)	(4)	(4)
(2)	(2)	(2)	(2)
Similar Industry/ Business	**Overall Risks**	**Focus**	**Ease of Implementation**
Points	Points	Points	Points
(13)	(16)	(16)	(10)
(8)	(13)	(13)	(8)
(6)	(6)	(10)	(6)
(4)	(4)	(4)	(4)
(2)	(2)	(2)	(2)
Operations	**Success Measurements**	**TOTAL POINTS**	**FINAL STRATEGY RANK**
Points	Points		
(12)	(10)	Opportunity A: ____	(1) ____
(10)	(8)	Opportunity B: ____	(2) ____
(6)	(6)	Opportunity C: ____	(3) ____
(4)	(4)	Opportunity D: ____	(4) ____
(2)	(2)	Opportunity E: ____	(5) ____

- **Overall risks.** To what extent does the opportunity avoid financial, operational, client, governmental, and competitive risks?
- **Focus.** Does the opportunity allow you to remain focused, and therefore not jeopardize your current business?
- **Ease of implementation.** Can you get things up and running easily and quickly?

- **Operations.** Does the opportunity exploit the same procedures as in your current business, or does it require you to develop new systems and operational steps?
- **Success measurements.** Will you be able to clearly measure the success of the initiative so that you can retreat if necessary?

4. Add up the points earned by each opportunity.

5. Based on total points earned, assign an overall ranking to your opportunities.

That's it! You've now put yourself in an optimal position to select and implement a growth opportunity that can bring you success.

Start It and Chart It

Y ou've planned, you've weeded out the weak, and you've chosen. Now it's time to move on to effective implementation of your initiative. It's time to get your timeline started. And by move, I mean *move*. Not "Let's get together and talk about it" or "Let me know when the first phase gets done." You've got to move *now,* and keep moving at a pace that's fast but effective. The longer you delay, the harder it is to get the plan moving. Lose momentum and the plan can stall—and then you leave potential profits on the table.

You've seen it before. Someone proposes a great idea. Everybody agrees it needs to get done, or at least looked into. The meeting breaks up and—lo and behold!—nothing happens. This is the way things go in 99.9 percent of the businesses I've been around.

The problem is the lack of accountability. When no one's butt is on the line to deliver the specific actions that need to get done, people just sit on their butts. But if you simply make someone accountable for a specific task, and everyone knows who's accountable for that task, things get done.

This principle transcends business; it's true in almost every facet of life. Your acknowledgment and understanding of it will give you a decided advantage as you set out to grow your business.

The Eight Elements of Action

So you're ready to get cracking on your new growth strategy. Where to begin? Here are the eight essential parts of a successful action plan, in more or less chronological priority:

1. The Team. When developing your action plan, include all the relevant departments and people within your business, regardless of its size. Do something to make them feel special as part of the team—give them T-shirts with the team name, present special plaques, hold team picnics. If it's a small company, include everybody; in a larger business, concentrate on the task force.

2. Leadership. Who will lead this new effort? In many cases, the owner. In the early, growth-filled years of my businesses, I'd lead the new effort to communicate priorities to my team. In a larger, more experienced company, you can put a trustworthy and well-organized top manager in charge, as long as you give her plenty of backup.

3. Organization. Map out a detailed operational process that will enable you to deliver on the new business. Analyze and cover every facet of the new processes. This might include getting more product, aligning with another business for increased capability (the way Sure Shot hooked up with eBay), or even restructuring the sales force to cover the new activity.

4. Current business. What do you need to do to keep current customers happy and feeling cared for? Be doubly careful not to drop the ball that's already in play; your existing business is the solid foundation on which the game of your growth depends.

5. Task timeline. Now that you understand the organizational processes you'll need for both your new and existing businesses, draw up a timeline of key action steps and critical dates. Include the names of the employees responsible for

Oh, You Mean Today?

Peter Martsmann and his team at Sure Shot Collectibles, the online collectibles marketplace, went through the same evaluation process we've just covered. They identified targets and white space opportunities, ranked their potential, and came up with two that made the grade: (1) they would grow vertically by expanding their product line to include jewelry, and (2) they would expand horizontally by linking their marketplace with eBay's hugely successful platform to reach new customers with all their products.

Now it was time to get started. Peter called a company kickoff meeting (always a solid idea) and outlined his vision. Everyone was psyched. Peter announced that Michele, a respected and long-tenured employee, would copilot the effort. The two met a few days later and drew up a comprehensive action list of things that needed to be done to succeed in the effort. The list was long, but they were confident they had all bases covered and that the plan would work. Michele met with her staff of three, and they talked with great commitment about what they should do next.

Four weeks later, Peter met with Michele and her group to get a progress report. "What's going on with everything?" he asked. "Fill me in." Blank stares. Nobody spoke a word.

No one had taken a single action on either project. Everyone thought someone else was on it. The net result? Less than zero. Four wasted weeks. What had promised to be a huge momentum builder for the company had morphed into an even bigger demotivator—bad for the employees, even worse for the business.

Whose fault was it? Peter and Michele's, for not managing the process to link specific tasks with specific persons. No one's butt was on the line. Great idea, great support up front, but no accountability.

Sure Shot eventually got their act together. They sat down and mapped out a detailed plan, then assigned individuals to each task. The result was, in the end, a successful endeavor, but the cost of the delay—which turned out to be five months longer than projected—was huge.

each step. Consult with these people to make sure the goals and dates are reasonable. When those who are accountable are involved in developing the plan, you'll get better buy-in.

Be realistic with your deliverable dates. If you're getting pushback from your employees or feel that they're sandbagging you—and that you cannot realistically meet your goals—you must reconsider the timeline, and perhaps even whether you should proceed with the initiative. Identifying and mitigating logistical risks up front can mean the difference between success and failure. Are you behind the eight ball before you even start? Not a good place to be.

6. Accountability. Assign every task that needs to be accomplished—from digging up market information and getting quotes to interviewing for new hires—to specific people if you're not handling them yourself; and get the names and tasks on paper. Use this schedule as a basis for regular status reports. This will help keep energy high and momentum at the right pitch. You'll find that once people are on the hook to perform, they rally to the cause. Review your timeline as often as possible and consult everyone on the project about whether and how well it's working; think of it as a working, breathing document.

> **Be doubly careful not to drop the ball that's already in play; your existing business is the solid foundation on which the game of your growth depends.**

I had great success using the following tactic. Once I had selected my team, I would hold a company meeting and post the task timeline, showing key deliverables, delivery dates, and who was responsible for each task. After the meeting I would post the task sheet where everybody could easily see it. The results were excellent. Deadlines were consistently met, and I never heard anyone say, "I didn't know I was supposed to do that."

My employees liked this system; it let everybody know how professional and effective the company considered them. If they also felt peer pressure—well, that was a bonus for the company. Each employee on the list shared the credit for the results.

7. Communication. Keep all employees informed about what's going on with the new business effort. A kickoff meeting is great, but only after you've set up your task

Here is a template I've used to monitor the implementation of new growth initiatives. In setting up the timeline, I've found it useful to begin at the end of the process and work backward. (But list them in chronological due date order.) That way it's easier to spot activities that affect other activities.

(Name of New Strategy Initiative)

Date:_____

Date Assigned	Action	Date Due	Person Responsible	Status

timeline at a preliminary meeting with the project leader and team so it can be shared with the entire company. At this meeting you should let all employees—*especially* if they aren't directly involved in the new venture—understand what this growth could mean to them. Let them know how crucial it is to keep the current business running well during the growth initiative. After the first meeting, it's usually enough to keep employees in the loop with e-mails sharing news of milestones reached.

Review your timeline as often as possible and consult everyone on the project about whether, and how well, it's working.

8. Measuring success. Any growth plan needs to be gauged continually for its effectiveness. If you're exceeding or falling short of your projections, you can rerun them and make the necessary adjustments—whether it means further expanding your capacity or chucking the whole effort. Of course you're going to succeed (you're following the advice in this book, after all), but if you can determine quickly that your new effort isn't working and that your core business is also in danger, shutting down the growth initiative quickly and refocusing on the base business can make the difference between surviving and succumbing. Live to fight another day.

You have many ways to track your progress. Hard numbers on sales and earnings are best, because they are real, not assumptions or estimates. Other measures, depending on your business, include the following:

- Tracking sales electronically through cash registers by coding new-item sales differently. Tabulate these daily for comparison with other sales.
- Creating new accounting codes to identify sales and invoices arising from new growth initiatives.
- Speaking with customers about your new initiative to see if it's working for them.
- Reporting sales and profits week to week or month to month for comparison with other years' numbers.
- Using an online metrics service, if you do Internet business, to track click-throughs, length of visit, and number of pages visited.
- Getting feedback from salespeople; employees on the front lines can usually tell you a lot about customer response. Although salespeople will hate it, you can ask them to fill out call sheets detailing specific experiences selling the new initiative to customers.

Regardless of which method you choose, it should give you real numbers that illuminate exactly how your new initiative is performing.

Best case: Your new initiative is making a profit, while your core operation continues to flourish. Keep it all going, and consider implementing an additional growth initiative.

Middle case: Your new initiative is struggling to break even or is losing money, while your core business continues to do well. Debug the new initiative if possible, but if unforeseen problems and unacceptable risks have come to light, dump it in a way that does no further damage—alienating old customers, for example—and then channel the resources into a new initiative.

Worst case: Despite your best efforts and a near-perfect initiative on paper, an unforeseeable change—for instance, in the interpretation of a government regulation—has thrown your new product or service offering into limbo, and no customers will risk using it until the uncertainty has been legally resolved. Not only is new business at a standstill, it's taking a toll on your core business. Revert to your old way of operating and, after the dust settles, explore a different growth strategy.

Few things can boost your business as effectively as choosing the ideal growth strategy and implementing it seamlessly. Now that you've selected your initiatives and determined how to measure their success, let's forge ahead.

Part V
CREATING VALUE

"Your task now is to help maximize and
communicate value to your customers to entice
them to buy your product."

The Method Behind the Madness

S o far, we've talked about preparing your business for growth by evaluating its soundness, harnessing the full potential of the sales force, and formulating solid growth strategies and tactics. As part of your business growth, there's something else you need to do: maximize the *value* of your products, your services, and your company as a whole.

Value is an intangible quality that a prospective customer assigns, often unconsciously, to something he's thinking of buying. If the product or service you are offering appears to have the "right" value, then you, my friend, have a sale.

Value may be a perception, but that doesn't mean it's not real. If you don't provide it, you'll jeopardize the success of your business. Every business should work diligently to maximize the value of its products and services. Why? Several reasons:

- Increased sales
- Higher profits
- Superior branding potential
- Longer company life
- Higher company valuation

Identifying, increasing, and maximizing value might seem like easy things to do, but, believe me, they're not. The art of figuring out how consumers connect that value to the "right" price—particularly since they're often not sure themselves—isn't easy. But that's what we're going to tackle in this part of the book. We'll start with understanding why customers buy from you, so that you can identify what they are seeking in terms of value. Then we'll move on to my methods for maximizing the value of your products and services.

> **Value is an intangible quality that a prospective customer assigns, often unconsciously, to something he's thinking of buying.**

A typical customer may take anywhere from seconds to months to decide how much a product is worth. He might not spend a lot of time deciding on a candy bar or a cup of coffee, but a car or an insurance policy? That's a different story. (Nonetheless, my daughter, Madison, can spend months picking out the perfect chocolate chip cookie, whereas my son Ryan will buy and eat any cookie at all, including the wrapper. You can make broad assumptions for the population as a whole, but the individual customer's needs and interests make the difference.)

Here's a chance to check your own value scale. Read the following list of consumer decisions and ask yourself how long it takes you to decide on the value of each:

- Which flavor of ice cream to get
- Which car to buy
- Which pack of mints to grab at the register
- Which magazine to buy at the airport
- Which pizza parlor you call to order pizza
- Which phone system to get for your office

- Which mobile phone service to use
- Which dry cleaner to patronize
- Which airline to fly
- What gift to get for a loved one's birthday

Even though you may consider yourself a typical customer, the decision-making process is uniquely personal. You may spend hours choosing the right watch; another buyer may make the decision in minutes. Your job as a business owner or salesperson is to shorten the decision-making process as much as possible. It's not easy, since most customers are in no hurry to shell out their hard-earned money. They need your help to rationalize and justify their decision to buy. That is, your job is:

> **Most customers are in no hurry to shell out their hard-earned money. They need your help to rationalize and justify their decision to buy.**

1. to help customers understand what their values are and see them in your product or service,

2. to create one or more unique selling propositions (USPs) that match the customer's values, and, finally,

3. to brand your products or services to readily communicate value to your customers. (More on this in part V, chapter 18.)

Why Customers Buy

By identifying the real reasons your customers buy what they buy, you'll be able to tailor your selling proposition (the "why" they should buy) to each customer base.

First, of course, you need to know which category your customers fit in.

You say you've never even thought of categorizing your customers? Well, what are you waiting for?

I divide customer needs into four categories. Remember that no category is inherently superior and that customers can shift from one category to another: A quality seeker at Macy's might be a price seeker at Blockbuster and a satisfaction seeker at Joe's Pizza Parlor. When customers decide whether to buy something, they are often motivated by more than one need.

To discover what motivates your customers:

- **Know your categories.** Read and understand each category definition below, especially the buzzwords and what each type of customer is thinking.
- **Gather intelligence.** Ask your customers why they buy. Develop a simple two- or three-question survey your sales or customer service personnel can use. Depending on your type of business, ask customers to rank their priorities: price? quality? style? selection? safety? If yours is a B2B, ask your salespeople to fill out the information based on their knowledge of customers and their purchases.
- **Get out and observe.** There's no substitute for your own eyes and ears. Walk your retail space; talk with customers; join a salesperson on a company call. Ask for opinions on how you're doing and how you can improve. You'll be surprised at how much people want to help you.

Four Categories of Customer

1. Quality seeker

2. Service seeker

3. Price seeker

4. Satisfaction seeker

Once you know what they're buying and why, you can generalize by putting customers into the four basic categories of need.

1. Quality seekers buy only when they find what they consider the best product out there. Price is secondary. They are savvy customers who comparison shop and research at length before they reach for their credit card. They want to know details about performance and materials— whatever makes your product or service the best.

Needs: The quality seeker wants to feel special—that she is getting the very best.

Buzzwords: Performance, materials

What she's thinking:

- In a specialty food store: What ingredients are used?
- At an executive search firm: How do they screen applicants?
- In a marketing company: What's the bottom-line result?
- At the dentist: Who are their referrals?
- With an online retailer: Which brand names are sold?

You can't lump your customers all into one group.

2. Service seekers need to feel you care about them, will do things for them, and won't forget them after they buy. Warranties, guarantees, and service are music to their ears. They want to know that any problems will be addressed right away.

Needs: The service seeker wants to be taken care of and acknowledged as significant.

Buzzwords: Convenience, customer service, warranties, and returns

What he's thinking:

- In a specialty food store: Can I find what I need and pay for it without standing in line? Do they deliver?
- At an executive search firm: What's my guarantee on candidates who are placed with us? What happens if they leave? Are they replaced?
- In a marketing company: Who will manage my account? Will she be open to my requests?
- At the dentist: Can I get a convenient appointment? Does the dentist run on schedule?
- With an online retailer: Is buying easy and painless? Can I return things I don't like? Is there online customer support?

3. Price seekers want to get the lowest price, even though they may be able to afford better quality and higher prices. The deal is what excites them. Businesses that guarantee to beat any competitor's price warm their hearts. For them, paying less than the next guy is a matter of pride.

Needs: The price seeker wants to feel she is a shrewd consumer.

Buzzwords: Lowest price, sale, discount

What she's thinking:

- In a specialty food store: If I buy two items, will I get the third for half off? Is there free gift-wrapping? Could I get the same item for less at a grocery store? Free delivery?
- At an executive search firm: If I find my own candidate, will the firm lower its rates?
- In a marketing company: Will the company reduce my rates if it fails to attract more business?
- At the dentist: How much will insurance pay? Are follow-up visits included in the price?
- With an online retailer: Does it offer online promotions and discounts? Is buying online cheaper than buying offline? Will I get a coupon for answering an online survey?

4. Satisfaction seekers are motivated by status, security, and the approval of others. These consumers are influenced strongly by the following factors:

The cool factor. The customer buys a product because it makes him feel part of the crowd. This is a powerful dynamic in the teen market, but adults fall prey to it as well—buying a particular brand of stroller for one's child, using a specific landscaping company, choosing where to go on vacation, or even buying a certain brand of beer because the right crowd drinks it.

The safety factor. The customer buys a product because he believes it will protect him or someone he cares about. Think of the Michelin tire slogan: "There's a lot riding on your tires." The safety-conscious family consumer is this company's target.

The job security factor. This factor emerges primarily when businesses buy products from other businesses.

Four Categories of Customer Need

Category	Buzzwords to Recognize	Customer Needs Solved
Quality seekers	Performance Quality	Feeling special Feeling that they are getting the best
Service seekers	Convenience Customer service Warranties and return	Feeling nurtured Being acknowledged as significant
Price seekers	Low price Sale Discount	Preserving or increasing status Feeling they are shrewd customers
Satisfaction seekers	Security Status Everybody has one	Feeling safe Feeling accepted

Corporate managers and executives tend to be wary of purchasing an unconventional product that may come back to haunt them. I often saw this fear in my marketing customers; potential clients accustomed to traditional programs like coupons were afraid they stood a greater chance of being penalized or even fired if my product didn't work.

Needs: The satisfaction seeker wants to feel safe and enjoy a sense of belonging.

Buzzwords: Security, status, everybody has one

What he's thinking:

- In a specialty food store: If I walk around with bags from this store, will people think I buy only the best?
- At an executive search firm: Should I use this firm even though my boss uses a different one?

- In a marketing company: If I buy this new service, will I be putting myself at risk with my bosses if it doesn't work out?
- With an online retailer: Does the site make me feel I'm joining the pioneers in the online world by embracing the latest technology?

Once you understand how your customers perceive value, you've laid the foundation for the next two steps in becoming an Elephant: developing the perfect unique selling proposition—and communicating it to the world.

What Makes You So Special?

Throughout my career, I have always strived to find out exactly why people purchased or rejected my products and services. I've learned a lot. I recognize that sometimes I made a sale because the buyer felt there was little risk. At other times, it was because my product seemed innovative and different from those offered by our competitors. Sometimes it was because the buyer liked the salesperson. Whatever the reason, I always tried to have my sales force tailor its presentations to fit my understanding of what my potential customers were looking for.

Your task now is to help your customers come to this value conclusion by creating one or more unique selling propositions (USPs). Then, through branding (the subject of next chapter), you can communicate the value to your customers in order to entice them to buy your product. USPs and branding give your sales force ways to objectify and quantify value. There are no better sales tools available.

What's a USP?

The unique selling proposition is the quality that makes your product or service rise above the rest. It can be something tangible—higher-quality ingredients, lower pricing, overnight delivery—or an abstraction, like a promise to make your life more fulfilling or your face younger-looking.

The perception of your USP is reality. That's right—the way it's perceived *is* the reality. What matters is that your USP motivates customers to put their hands in their wallets by appealing deeply, even unconsciously, to one or more of their needs. It is likely that within your products or services you already possess all you need in order to develop and communicate effective USPs. What you have to do is uncover these hidden USPs, package them, and use branding to present them to the prospect. The more creatively you can do this, the better your chances of making the sale and growing your business.

USPs are all around you. Here are some familiar, successful ones.

Company	USP	How Used
Nike	Inner strength, motivation	"Just do it."
AT&T	Impact someone's life by telephoning	"Reach out and touch someone."
Burger King	Customer choice	"Have it your way."
Bounty paper towels	Quality, convenience	"The quicker picker-upper."
Federal Express	Speedy, reliable delivery	"When it absolutely, positively has to be there overnight."

When to Create USPs

As important as knowing *how* to create a USP is knowing *when* to create one. Developing a USP can save a sale, a client, or even an entire company whenever one of these five scenarios arises:

1. When your product or service is better than your competition's. You can never go wrong by drawing attention to your product's advantages over the competitors'. In fact, anytime your service has an advantage in an area of importance to your customer, you must promote that advantage.

Consider Sure Fire Collectibles, a company that specializes in buying and selling products through online auctions. Ryan Rausus, its owner, started the company three years ago as a hobby. Now it's a full-time job. To understand the marketplace better, Ryan consistently visits, monitors, and audits the websites run by his competition.

He realized that Sure Fire has a faster inventory turnaround time than any of his competitors. His buyers usually receive their goods in a couple of days. His competitors' customers can wait weeks. Ryan developed a USP around this competitive advantage. He named it the Sure Fire Delivery Guarantee, a distinctive brand he promoted in all his marketing, advertising, and sales materials.

2. When your competition is better than you are in a critical area. If your business has a weak spot in an area important to your customers, develop a USP to mitigate your competitors' advantage.

Tim Redia owns Take Two Video, a video rental store in Los Angeles situated less than two miles from a huge video megastore. Like any small store, Take Two couldn't promise as wide a selection as its gargantuan counterpart.

Tim decided to create a USP around the issue of availability by guaranteeing that new releases would be in stock. To make good on his promise, he networked with other

Five Reasons to Create a USP

1. When your product or service is better than your competition's.

2. When your competition is better than you are in a critical area.

3. When you hear the same objections to your product over and over.

4. When you discover your customers' hot spots.

5. When you need to persuade a target audience why you're right for them.

small video stores outside the neighborhood. They agreed to fight the big boys by exchanging video inventory if any of them ran low on a particular title.

Tim promoted his USP through in-store signage, local newspapers, and fliers. As a result, he's been able to keep his small store off the cutting-room floor.

3. When you hear the same objections to your product over and over. USPs are a great way to preempt the complaints and objections you consistently hear from your customers.

My marketing firm specialized in distributing product samples directly to consumers on behalf of companies like Procter & Gamble and the Hershey Company. Because we delivered millions of product samples to consumers throughout the nation, customers were always worried about whether we'd be effective at receiving the samples, repackaging them along with other items like informational brochures, then shipping them directly to distribution points such as schools and hospitals.

Weighing against us were the expense of the samples and our relative inexperience. No matter how many hours I spent trying to persuade potential customers that we could handle the job, they remained skeptical.

One day I sat down with my seven employees to develop a USP based on perfection in packaging and shipping. First we met with shipping companies that transported our products, like United Parcel Service. Then we came up with a plan to include a special label with a UPC bar code on each box we shipped out. To reassure our customers that all deliveries were being made, we'd enable them to go online and track their packages.

We called the new program SampleTrak™. The name spoke for itself. I distributed a one-page SampleTrak sell sheet to our prospective clients. They reacted immediately. Not only did people stop citing shipping concerns, but many clients started calling us the gold standard in sample delivery, a reputation that burnished my company's image in the marketplace.

By the way, if the SampleTrak program sounds strangely familiar, it's because all we did was to give our own nickname—and spin—to the tracking system already in place at United Parcel Service. We persuaded the shipper to let us affix the SampleTrak trademark to our United Parcel Service labels, then gave our clients our tracking password. To make this unique selling proposition a grand slam, the entire program was done at no cost to us, and UPS gave us the label printers to boot. As a tradeoff, UPS received most of our shipping business.

4. When you discover your customers' hot spots. Few things are as valuable as knowing what your customers really want.

Dom Semaudy is president of Blue Chip Electronics, a local electronics store in a suburban Detroit strip mall that specializes in everyday needs. To stave off competition from the superstores, Dom stays very attuned to his clientele, in part by asking them what they like and don't like about their experiences in other electronic stores.

Through these conversations, Dom became privy to his customers' hot button: service. They loved the attention he gave them and the assurance that, when they walked into the store, someone would help them find what they needed.

Dom sprang into action and developed a USP around the service motif. He called the quick, friendly service he provided The Blue Chip Experience. He promoted his Blue Chip promise throughout the community and leveraged it against his competition, implying that the electronic superstores were far too large to really care about their customers.

5. When you need to persuade a target audience why you're right for them. Andi Paknal, a massage therapist, is the president of Just Relax Massages, a one-woman business she operates out of a Texas beauty salon. Because of her extensive training in the field, Andi expected to have many clients. Her specialty was pain relief and deep-tissue massage with a focus on athletes. Her problem was a limited clientele—her current customers were mostly women who sought massages only to relieve stress. Since her business was in a beauty salon, the athletes she wanted to target wouldn't give her a second look.

Creating a USP

1. List your rationale for creating a USP.

2. Determine the customer category you're trying to satisfy.

3. Develop potential USPs.

4. Select the best USP.

The USP Andi developed to tackle this problem and win them over was a product that combined several disciplines of massage therapy into a sixty-minute session including reflexology, deep-tissue massage, and stretching. She branded this new product Sports Therapy. Then she distributed a promotional flyer at athletic hangouts, like gyms and sporting events.

Andi's idea took off. When we last spoke, her calendar was full and she'd hired two more therapists to help her with the overflow.

Creating the Perfect USP

Once you've analyzed your customers' needs to find out how best to approach them (which we did in the last chapter), then analyzed your business's need for a USP, it's time to pull everything together. I use a simple but effective series of steps to draw up a USP-creation chart that helps me organize my efforts:

Step 1: List your rationale for creating a USP. Use my list of Five Reasons to Create a USP to guide you here. List only the categories that apply to your case. For example, if you own a marketing company, and a potential customer asks whether its promotional materials, product samples, and

USP Creation Chart

Situation (USP Rationales)
Consistent customer objection: concern that the client's samples won't reach their destination.

offers would actually reach the hands of its intended consumers, you might focus on a USP for delivery.

Step 2: Determine the customer category you're trying to satisfy. Next to each rationale, indicate the relevant customer needs. Using the information you gathered from the previous chapter, identify the appropriate category of need for the customer at whom you are aiming the USP. If more than one type of customer is being targeted, include all applicable categories.

USP Creation Chart

Situation (USP Rationales)	Customer Needs Category
Consistent customer objection: concern that the client's samples won't reach their destination.	Quality seeker Satisfaction seeker (job security)

Step 3: Develop potential USPs. Treat this step as if you were solving a riddle. Be creative and thorough. For each rationale, ask yourself which of your company's elements or operations might solve the problem. Then comb through each one of these features. Before you know it, you'll have a list of potential USPs.

When potential customers of my marketing company started questioning our ability to ship properly, I consulted not only the shipping and packing departments but also the market research and accounting departments. From that feedback came the idea of the SampleTrak USP.

Looking at the details of how your company operates can also be fruitful. Pay special attention to the ways you do things, from how you make your product to how you deliver it and bill for it. Take another look at the material on operational mandates in part IV, chapter 13. This will help you identify these problem-solving elements.

You may be surprised to find your USP right under your nose. For example, a friend of mine, Jim Schubert, owns a small accounting firm. He developed a USP around what he calls Client One, his method of reviewing tax returns with an eye toward reducing his clients' tax burden. Client One has brought Jim countless new clients. What's interesting is that the Client One method is what Jim has always done for his clients—he just made it a USP, branded it, and promoted it.

Use the list below to begin thinking about how the various departments of your company might give birth to potential USPs, or how your existing products and services might be repackaged as a USP. Be sure to consult with other people in your company as you eliminate unworthy candidates for your USP. By engaging others in the process, you're enlisting their support of the USP, and you may find it good policy to select one or more of them to implement it.

USP Creation Chart

Situation (USP Rationales)	Customer Needs Category	Potential USPs
Consistent customer objection: concern that the client's samples won't reach their destination.	Quality seeker Satisfaction seeker	*Accounting method:* Use billing audits to verify delivery by checking with facilities that actually shipped the samples. Adjust client invoices for any missing deliveries. *Market research:* Screen the targeted recipients for receipt after delivery. *Legal:* Guarantee delivery through bidding customer contracts. Provide refunds and other remedies for undelivered items. *Shipping method:* Coordinate with United Parcel Service's delivery system and implement real-time access to delivery status.

Step 4: Select the best USP. Okay, you've got candidates. In order to select the ideal USP, run each of the potential USPs through the following six tests and rule out those that don't pass.

1. Response to rationale. There's no other way to determine how well your proposed USP responds to the customer's need other than thinking through the details. Here's how the analysis played out in my sample shipping example:

- **Accounting method.** Auditing the receipt of packages might seem to solve the delivery problem, because billing could be adjusted after the fact. Yet it wouldn't respond to what the clients are really concerned about: that the samples reach the consumers in the first place. Paying less for undelivered samples is of secondary concern, so the accounting solution to the USP is not going to make the final cut.
- **Market research.** This option also deals with the receipt of the samples after the fact. Scratch it off the list.
- **Legal.** Affording clients a legal right to delivery might put their concerns to rest. It bespeaks a level of commitment not promised by the accounting or market-research options. The legal option survives, for now.
- **Shipping method.** Coordinating with the proven delivery services is just what the client would want; it alleviates the client's concerns in advance. This makes the cut as well.

Now we move on to test two, with legal and shipping the only USP options remaining.

2. Response to customer needs. Consider whether either of the surviving USP options can satisfy the customer needs you've identified:

- **Legal.** The customers here are quality seekers, satisfaction seekers, and price seekers. The binding contract appeals to price seekers because they're assured of paying for only what is delivered. The legal option also appeals to the quality seekers because it suggests we're willing to put our hides on the line to deliver. Satisfaction seekers can take comfort in having legal cover for their backsides.

- **Shipping method.** Partnering with a well-known outfit like United Parcel Service would satisfy the quality seekers by enhancing our credibility and providing an online, real-time status report. Satisfaction seekers will also be reassured by the association with an accepted, well-regarded outfit like United Parcel Service. For the price seekers, I would emphasize that verifying delivery with the shipping companies will ensure the customers aren't charged for undelivered samples.

3. Ease of implementation. Now it's time to consider the logistics of implementing your options. Many times I have come up with promising USPs, only to discover that they were a pipe dream at best. The trick here is to look at each potential USP and figure out exactly what it will take to make it a reality.

- **Legal.** Although it might be easy to add a delivery guarantee to our customer contracts, it would be much harder to abide by those terms. Still, since the ultimate goal is to ensure delivery, we should be willing to do what it takes to perform. The legal option moves along.
- **Shipping method.** Since we are already using United Parcel Service, the implementation centers more on how to include our customers in the process. We would need to negotiate with United Parcel Service over how to use our custom labels and allow our clients access to our online account. Shipping proceeds to the next step as well.

4. Time frame. The next test is to determine how long it would take to implement the USP option. If you have a great potential USP but it's going to take you a year to implement, it may or may not be worth your while. For this step, fully define a timetable for the USP.

- **Legal.** We estimate that it would take about a month to work through the details behind our guarantee—an acceptable time frame for us.
- **Shipping method.** We allow three to four months to negotiate with United Parcel Service, print our shipping labels to include the UPC codes, and register our customers for online account usage, a bit longer than the legal option but still acceptable.

5. Cost. At this pivotal stage, make sure to include all aspects of creating and implementing the USP, particularly such hidden costs as legal fees and other professional expenses, increases in manufacturing time, opportunity costs that may arise, and the workforce needed to deliver on the USP.

- **Legal.** We estimate the actual legal costs to be only about $1,500, the fee for revising our current standard contract. But what about the inevitable hidden costs? For example, we expect that about 2 percent of the samples wouldn't be delivered. Therefore, we would have to refund 2 percent on every contract. We'd also need to designate a full-time employee to run the auditing and refunds. In the end, the cost would be about $100,000—a great burden for my business. However, because we believe the USP might attract significant new business, I decide to keep the legal option at hand.
- **Shipping method.** The actual cost of shipping the samples would remain unchanged, as would the cost of the labels. We even anticipate a slight reduction in our shipping rates, since we would now be giving virtually all of our shipping business to United Parcel Service. The cost of getting our clients online would be negligible.

There's a thin line between unique and realistic.

The only real costs would be the additional manpower needed to monitor the labeling and tracking operations, and the cost of promoting our new tracking service to prospective clients. When reduced by the savings in shipping costs, estimated net cost is under $10,000.

6. Risks. The final test requires you to forecast risk. Make sure to consider the following:

- **Impact on your customer.** Will your customers embrace the new USP? Will some reject it?
- **Liabilities, exposure, and litigation.** Could this USP increase your legal liability? Are you making claims that could put you in a legal mess if you fail to deliver?
- **Internal concerns.** How might the USP affect company culture? Will you need to promote or reposition employees to deliver on the USP?
- **Downside.** If the USP doesn't work, what's the worst-case scenario?

Here's how the two remaining USPs shape up after taking into account possible risk factors:

- **Legal.** The contract option is riddled with risks. By guaranteeing to refund undelivered samples, we'd be committing ourselves to a monitoring process that could last far into the future. And under the binding contract, we'd be subject to potential liability and legal action even if disaster struck beyond our control. With a small company like mine, one honest mistake could put us out of business.

Another risk is the downside potential. The worst-case scenario, besides being destroyed by litigation, would be implementing an elaborate contract without attracting any new business. All we'd reap for our efforts is a 2 percent reduction in revenues because of the refunds. Suddenly, the legal option isn't looking so good.

- **Shipping method.** Here the risks are minimal. Since the labeling option won't really change the way we're operating, internal concerns don't enter the picture. Litigation and exposure seem unlikely, because we aren't promising to do anything more or less than what we were doing before. The biggest downside would be if our efforts didn't create any new business—a risk we are willing to take.

So the shipping USP it is! The verdict may not always be this clear, but using this method of selecting a USP is the only path to a logical, positive choice.

Now it's time to communicate the value of this USP to your customers. Say hello to branding!

The Name Game

I could write a whole book on branding alone. In fact, many others have. But my goal here isn't to teach you a classroom curriculum on branding. Rather, it's to focus on just one aspect of branding: what you need to know, right now, to quickly increase the value of your business and products. That is, naming the value developed by the USP in order to communicate that value to your customer. Although there's more to branding than this, I'll risk the ire of marketing experts by boldly using the familiar word *brand* instead of the awkward term *name of your USP*.

Your objective is to create a name for your distinctive product, service, attribute, or process—along with an aura of quality, value, or status—and make your target customer familiar with it. This brand name communicates the identity and personality of your USP. If you succeed, your brand name or logo will instill an expectation, a feeling of desire, a perception of value, in any prospect who sees it.

Singing Your Own Praises

Skillful branding can make ordinary products or services more successful than the superior but unbranded or poorly branded products. A quick tour of any grocery store proves my point. When you see a generic brand or the grocery store name on a product, what do you think is in the package? A lesser-quality product, right? Wrong—usually it's the same cereal, cookies, cough medicine, or coffee creamer as the leading brand. Often the manufacturer of the leading brand produces it for the stores, then simply packages it with the store brand or a generic label for a lower price. When the shelf label says, "Compare with the leading brand," you can take it literally. Check out the ingredients; it's usually the fancy product in everyday dress.

Seven Steps to Developing Your Brand

1. List USP details.

2. Convert details to pops.

3. Review customer needs.

4. Compile a working list.

5. Test names.

6. Select *the* name.

7. Promote the name.

But here's what happens. Because most people feel the need to buy "quality," or to avoid the perceived stigma of the low-income-targeted product, they would rather pay more for the branded product than pay less for the *exact same product* without the brand. That's the power of branding—and human nature!

Here's an example of how branding works. Susan Johnson, who owns a local dry cleaning store, heard many customers complain that dry cleaning often left their clothes rough and uncomfortable. Johnson didn't simply solve the problem; she took advantage of it by making her customers' need—softer clothes—her USP, and then branding it. She called her new service Eversoft Comfort Enzymes. The new brand identity embodied exactly what customers wanted and gave them a name to grab onto. By increasing the amount of softener in her cleaning formula, Susan was able to deliver on this promise. She posted signs around her store and created a one-page brochure explaining and promoting Eversoft, placing a pile of them on the counter for her customers.

This is a great example of how good branding works. Susan took a customer dissatisfaction seriously and branded the solution memorably and credibly.

Do-It-Yourself Branding

You can, as I've done in the past, hire expensive agencies to brand your products or services, but in most cases you can do it yourself. After all, who knows your market and product better than you do? It's not that hard if you do it systematically. Here's the process I use, in seven easy steps:

1. List USP details. The first step in branding your USP is to jot down as many details as you can about your USP—what it does, how it works, what it stands for. SampleTrak, for example, features ways to:

- allay customers' concerns about whether their samples will be delivered,
- track the delivery of samples,
- allow customers to access their inventory, and
- use technology as the next-generation solution to delivering samples.

2. Convert details to pops. Pops are punchy, reductive descriptions of the details. Create as many pops as you like. Consider the following examples:

- Process, quality, fulfillment
- Sample delivery tracking
- Customer inventory access
- Hi-tech

3. Review customer needs. List the customer needs relevant to the USP, be they the needs of quality seekers, price seekers, or satisfaction seekers.

4. Compile a working list. Here's where you get creative. Start juggling and combining the details, pops, and customer needs to generate a working list of potential names for your USP. Don't worry about having too many names—at this point, the more the merrier. Look for names that respond to your customers' needs and give your USP personality and identity. Don't censor yourself; off-the-wall names often work as well as technical ones. For each USP, shoot for at least twenty names on your working list.

Do You Need a Trademark?

Once you have identified your USP and designated a brand name, you've actually created a trademark for the product. Trademarking your USP creates legal rights that can be enforced both locally and nationwide.

In general, the first person to use a trademark in connection with the product owns the rights to the mark. Many business owners simply add the trademark symbol (™) themselves and claim it as a trademark. If your business is small and you don't really care about infringements, this may be all the protection you need. However, if you're heavily invested in your USP or will lose a lot of money if someone "borrows" your brand name, or if you believe that having a trademark symbol adorn the name will provide some cachet to your product, consider registering the trademark officially. A federal trademark registration provides many advantages, such as the right to include your mark in a central trademark registry, thus alerting others to your rights—and ownership.

Before you finalize the name for your USP, conduct a trademark search to determine whether anyone is already using the name. You can perform your own informal federal trademark search simply by visiting **www.nameprotect.com** or by going directly to the United States Trademark Office's website, **www.uspto.gov.** If you believe a formal search is necessary, a patent or trademark attorney can consult a comprehensive computer data service. This search should cost you less than $1,000. The attorney can also help you apply for a federal trademark registration at a modest cost of $400 to $600, plus a filing fee of approximately $350. Correspondence with the trademark office could add an additional $1,000 to the cost.

If you're not using the name nationwide but only within a state, many states let you register under a state trademark act at a lower cost.

5. Test names. Get people's reactions to your names. Poll customers and prospects. What comes to mind when they hear each name? Scramble the order of the names occasionally so that the same ones aren't always first on your list.

6. Select the name. Now it's time to choose the best name. Review the criteria so that you're comfortable with your decision.

7. Promote the name. Market and advertise the brand to your customers. Use it on sales materials, sales pitches, and websites. In fact, use it everywhere. Promote it internally so that all your employees, not just sales, can rally around it.

By developing and branding USPs, you create value that extends far beyond the customers you serve, value that you can use to gain more customers and that enables you to command a higher price if you ever sell your company. Having bought and sold many businesses, I can tell you that the businesses that command the highest price are those with the highest perceived value in the customer's mind. And achieving that value is the job of USPs and brand identity.

The Strategic Alliance Puzzle

We've come a long way toward growing your business, but the process isn't complete until we address one of the most common and most effective methods of growing with minimum investment and risk: the strategic alliance.

Strategic alliances give your business the opportunity to grow by providing more products and services to more customers than you can offer on your own. You get these capabilities by aligning with another company. A *strategic alliance* is an agreement with one or more other entities to conduct certain kinds of business together for mutual benefit, under specific terms. Virtually any business of any size can form a successful alliance.

Strategic alliances take many forms. Often they are simple, non-contractual agreements between businesses to work toward a common goal or to address market demand in the most effective way possible. One form this agreement can take is between coequal partners, with the businesses contributing similar amounts of

Strategic alliances give your business the opportunity to grow by providing more products and services to more customers than you can offer on your own.

resources, dividing the authority and responsibility, sharing the expenses, and splitting the profits. This form of alliance is intrinsically unstable, because one partner or the other tends to become dominant.

Another type of strategic alliance is the consortium, in which two or more businesses cooperate but one business takes the lead. The "front" company might set strategy and own the relationship with the customer, while the others might provide products or services that the lead company adds to its line and sells to its customer. There are many varieties of consortiums with different degrees of participation. It's up to you to decide what works best for your business.

The Consortium

Of the many forms a strategic alliance can take, my favorite is the consortium. Of course, the partner I want to be is the dominant partner (Company Alpha in the diagram opposite). This way, I own the relationship with the customer, giving me leverage over my consortium partners. On the other hand, you may prefer at times to be a subordinate partner, handing over the organization, marketing, and sales responsibilities (and a lot of the headaches) to the dominant partner and concentrating on the operations that you do best.

There are several ways to structure a consortium deal, but perhaps the simplest and most effective is one in which the customer buys only from you. You then pass the order to one of your partners, who executes it on your behalf. Your partner stays out of sight, while the customer gets what he wants: seamless service. You do the billing, and when you receive payment, you take out your share for the services you provide, plus the markup or commission, and pass the rest to your consortium partner.

Because you now have more capabilities, this alliance may enable you to go after many more customers than if you were

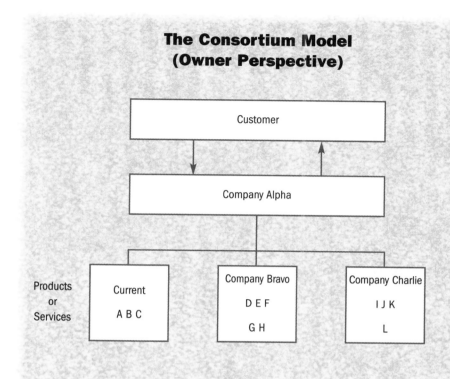

The Consortium Model
(Owner Perspective)

operating alone, or perhaps sell more to the same customer—yet you maintain control of the customer relationships. In almost all cases it yields higher margins; you receive revenue for activities that cost you little or nothing because others perform them.

But what does the consortium model look like from the viewpoint of sales staff and customers? As we noted, service will appear seamless to the customer in a smoothly operating consortium; whether the product or service is received directly from you or from one of your partners will make no difference. Depending on the type of consortium, salespeople get access to a much larger catalog of products they can sell to meet the needs of customers, and they gain opportunities to sell to new and bigger customers as well. Customers typically experience better service, higher quality, or lower prices.

The key word here is "seamless." That is, neither

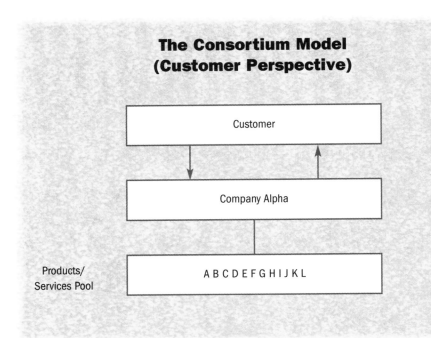

The Consortium Model (Customer Perspective)

Customer

Company Alpha

Products/Services Pool

A B C D E F G H I J K L

For many egotistical souls in the business community, self-reliance and individualism are too often treated as givens.

the customer nor the salesperson should notice whether the product or service in question is one of your core services or a service you are now getting from a consortium partner. That's how smooth it should be. One exception: There might be a situation in which you wish to take advantage of a partner's reputation for product quality, service, or credibility. In this case you could hope to improve your prospects of a sale (or perhaps command a higher price) by promoting your alliance with this partner to your prospect.

To Ally or Not to Ally

When does it make sense to form a strategic alliance? For many egotistical souls in the business community, self-reliance and individualism are too often treated as givens. The idea of having a partner is anathema, and joining forces with another company is not much higher on one's list of things to do. But in the modern marketplace, a strategic alliance offers great advantages, especially in the following situations:

- When you need to have a bigger business proposition to either (1) realize more profits from a larger total order (part of something bigger), or (2) compete for bigger orders, projects, customers, contracts, or RFPs (requests for proposals).

- When you want to compete against bigger competitors.

- When you need to fulfill an operational shortfall.

- When you need to limit your risk exposure while expanding into another service or industry.

- When you want to grow but can't raise the money to finance it.

- When you desire to expand internationally and need in-market expertise.

- When you're considering buying or selling to another company and need a way to test each other out. (I prefer this when I'm buying a business, not selling one, because once you partner up it becomes hard to separate if the match isn't working, and this can leave clients and employees in limbo.)

Even the most self-reliant Elephant needs a partner sometimes.

Think of every aspect of your business and ask yourself whether you can improve it through a partnership. You can specify your own terms. Try for an alliance that doesn't require you to invest cash; many alliances don't involve up-front money but benefit both partners because the combined total revenues and profits increase.

For example:

- Your firm invests money for high-net-worth individuals but mostly sells stocks and municipal bonds. If you form an alliance with an insurance broker, you may be able to sell insurance to your current clients and receive a commission from the insurance company on their new premiums.

- Your company installs and repairs heating and air-conditioning systems. You align with an electrical contractor, form a pitch team, and go after large community developers.

- You publish an online magazine and are in need of solid content, which typically costs you a lot of money. You offer the cachet and large readership of your online magazine in exchange for content written by another person or organization.

- You make space available for your partner's inventory in exchange for their help in selling your goods.

- You exchange technologies with a noncompeting business for mutual benefit.

Take a close look at how the alliance would affect your potential partners. What would they get from the arrangement? Don't be shy about selling the idea to them; outline the advantages to their firm as well as the advantages to yours. This sets the stage for a discussion of the logistics. (Note to negotiators: If there's a big upside for you, but it's not obvious, don't bring it up. Your potential partner might use it as leverage for a better deal.)

> **Don't be shy about selling the idea; outline the advantages to their firm as well as the advantages to yours.**

Protect Yourself!

Imagine that you have formed a strong, effective alliance. Business is booming, you and your new partner are working shoulder to shoulder, and everybody's making money. Then, suddenly, all hell breaks loose and you and your partner become the Hatfields versus the McCoys. The consortium is

Strategic Alliances Chart

The following chart illustrates how several companies have enhanced their offerings by forming strategic alliances with other companies. In each of these cases the alliance provided mutual benefit to each business:

Company	Partner	Current Capability	Enhanced by Alliance
Bill's Pizza	Star Power	Pizza in & delivery	One source—deliver pizza & movie
Insignia Pops	Valassis, Inc.	Promotions in stores	Promotions in newspapers
Sam Richards Assoc.	Hybrid Corp.	Loans—remodeling	Loans—new construction
SCA	National Safety Council	Magazine editorial— fun	Magazine editorial— safety
Carole McVey Assoc.	Robert Sims Insurance	Wealth management/ stocks and bonds	Insurance
Aunt Jamie's Cookies	Yan's Gifts & Cakes	Homemade cookies/ baked goods and a card	One source—cards, cookies, & cakes for all occasions
Global Healthcare	Various health-care cos.	Management	Diagnostics
Barnes & Noble	Starbucks	Book sales	Increased traffic: buy a book, have coffee
Live for Success	Steve Rogers, Business Expert	Life coaching	Enhance credibility & get business advice
Nicetickets.com	TicketsUK.uk	Online ticket broker	Enhanced ticket inventory— international
ADT Engineering	ABCO Design	Building highways	Added capability to pursue government contracts

in danger of breaking apart. What have you done to protect yourself financially, ethically, and legally?

If you're smart, you will have addressed each of the following issues before you embark on any alliance:

- Make sure you have a written agreement outlining the details of the alliance, including remedies for breach of the agreement, and addressing what would happen in the event that either party wishes to split the bedsheets and move on.

- Know who will own the customer relationship, both contractually and pragmatically. Will this alliance put you at risk with your existing customers? Will you have access to your partner's customer base? Can you write legal protection into your alliance agreement?

- Work out the detailed sales and operational processes.

- Make sure you can fulfill your end of the deal without giving away the keys to the kingdom. When you discuss the operating process with your prospective partner, don't hand over any proprietary processes or work products.

- Know who owns the relationship with the suppliers. If it's not you, can you get new suppliers quickly?

- Make sure you can work together while keeping the entities separate, both physically and emotionally. This will help avoid hits to employee morale and give you better control over your company culture.

- Determine who controls the billing. The one who controls the cash is in the driver's seat, regardless of any contract.

- Specify how sales commissions will be structured. The last thing you want is angry salespeople. A true alliance will give all parties an opportunity to make more money—especially the sales force. If this isn't happening, make sure your guys are covered. Often what happens is that salespeople are asked to sell additional items to their customers and split the commissions on sales from the alliance partner; just make sure they aren't selling the same or more while making less. They will all feel resentful if you don't address the issue.

- Communicate all these issues to your entire company. Don't leave anything to their imagination. If you do, chances are they'll think of the worst scenario and focus on that.

Part VI
KILLER MISTAKES

"The single most important reason
why growing businesses crash
is the failure to develop the processes
needed to handle that growth
in the first place."

Failing to Lead

D an Plakani owned Team Excellence, a consulting firm offering sales training to companies and individuals. In addition to training sessions, he and eleven associates sold books, tapes, DVDs, and other materials, both online and off. Business was slow at first, but new and repeat customers pumped up annual revenues to over $1 million after three years. This was largely due to Dan's own efforts; like many of us, he spent thirty-six hours a day on his business, brought in most of the clients, and ran operations as well.

As Team Excellence prospered, Dan hired more people. At the same time, he wisely set up processes to ensure timely and efficient completion and delivery on sales. He kept working at an inhuman pace. After five years, he hit it big—three new clients, all giant companies. Team Excellence was now in the big leagues, with sales of $8 million and profits over $2 million. As if that wasn't enough, Dan wrote a book that quickly became a bestseller.

Dan began spending most of his time doing interviews to promote his book and his company. He relished his time in the spotlight, but more important, it was a welcome break from the pressures of his business. Having built an organization that handled the sales and operations, and having installed a new president at the helm, he finally felt able to relax and catch his breath.

Then he got the e-mail. From his best salesperson. Subject line: "Are you kidding me?" Contents: excerpts from e-mails that the new president had shotgunned to all employees. One praised the new brand of office coffee.

No matter how successful your business becomes, your job as the leader never disappears. It only evolves.

Another urged employees to use every page of their legal pads before discarding them. These were followed by messages rating local restaurants and threatening employees who left dirty dishes in the sink.

Because of the integrity of his salesperson, Dan knew this wasn't just an attempt to show the boss in a bad light. Then he saw the real bomb in her e-mail: "We're growing like crazy and need some leadership."

It dawned on Dan that his company had been rudderless for more than six months. Not only was he in danger of losing his best salesperson, his fast-growing out-of-control company was in danger of blowing up. The issue, of course, was not dirty dishes in the office sink (although the fact that the new president concerned himself with such trivia was a bad sign). The real problem was that employees needed to know that their leader was in the trenches with them, helping them meet the challenges of growth—especially with the founder (Dan) off somewhere chasing other dragons. The president's frivolous e-mails left little doubt that he was in over his head.

Before the damage could be repaired, several big clients became disenchanted and left. In less than a year, sales in the once-growing company had fallen below $4 million.

Whose fault was this? As you might guess, the fault was mostly Dan's. He had neglected his own responsibility as a leader. He had been so happy to get away from the daily pressures of the business that he lost sight of how he had made the company so successful. Although the thought of taking up the daily workload again made him ill, Dan had no choice. His beloved company was sinking, and it might have gone under had he not been alerted in time. The reality was a much-needed slap in the face, and he recovered with renewed fervor. He encouraged the president to pursue career opportunities elsewhere, then climbed back into the captain's chair.

It took a couple of years of damage repair, but Team Excellence recovered and regained nearly all of its lost ground. Dan has stayed focused on the business, and it is now doing well. He has also come to a new realization: No matter how successful your business becomes, your job as the leader never disappears. It only evolves.

Lonely at the Top

Although I have always thought of myself as someone who could rally people around a common goal, I had to learn the true meaning of leadership the hard way. Some of the best lessons are about what leadership is *not*.

Being an owner and being a leader are not the same. Owners can hire and fire at will and order people around, but that does not make them leaders. I've also seen business owners try to pal around with their employees rather than lead them, an approach that can have the same disastrous effect as tyrannical managing.

Although leadership can be rewarding, it's not always glamorous. Yes, it definitely is lonely at the top, especially when it's time to make a critical decision. Your employees can help, but they can't decide for you; your friends and family support you, but they aren't familiar with the issues; networking

> **Being an owner and being a leader are not the same.**

with other professionals has its limits. You often find yourself sacrificing money, attention, and popularity to do what's best for your company's long-term success, especially when you're growing.

Five Keys to Leadership in a Growing Company

Entrepreneurs, almost by definition, are driven, but the truly successful are those who motivate and inspire others to push beyond their limits. From my own experience and that of other successful leaders I've known, I've distilled the following keys to effective leadership during times of company growth. Although leadership styles may vary, following these precepts will keep your train on the tracks.

1. Lead by example. Your employees will take their cues from what you do, not what you say. If you demand long hours but walk out the door at noon, how seriously will people take you? When I was running my businesses hands-on, I often left e-mails or voice mails for employees after midnight and on weekends. I also let it be known that when I wasn't at work I spent plenty of time with my family. They got the message—and soon followed my lead. The result was a culture of hard work in a family environment.

Leading by example goes far beyond the hours you keep; it defines your company's personality. Do you treat your employees with respect or with suspicion? Do your employees hear you working out how best to serve customers or how to chisel a few extra bucks out of them? Do you make fun of employees behind their backs or praise them to their peers? Do you follow up on your plans and orders or issue and forget? Do you keep your promises or look for loopholes? Your employees, for their part, will mirror your tone and demeanor when interacting with other employees, clients, suppliers, and customers.

Five Keys to Leadership

1. Lead by example.

2. Be consistent.

3. Be approachable.

4. Maintain the home front.

5. Excel during adversity.

2. Be consistent. Your employees need to know what to expect from you. If you're rational one day and volatile the next, or if you change the rules of the game without warning or apparent reason, those you're trying to lead may become confused and ineffective. Being consistent calms the anxiety that builds up under the pressure of growth. If they know how you're going to react, they can adjust their actions to meet your expectations.

3. Be approachable. Whether you have one employee or one thousand, it's a huge mistake to isolate yourself. Every Monday I would wander down to the mailroom and strike up a conversation with Phil, the mailroom clerk, about sports, weather, or current events—just small talk. Phil's job took him to all departments, all employees. He was very social, tuned in to the pulse of the company; everybody liked him and enjoyed chatting with him. I enjoyed Phil's company, too, but aside from that, I learned more about my employees' concerns during those impromptu five-minute sit-downs than I ever could from an hour-long meeting with my managers. What Phil knew about the concerns of the rank and file simply would never have filtered up the management chain on its own.

> **Leading by example goes far beyond the hours you keep; it defines your company's personality.**

I once asked a renowned Chicago surgeon the secret to his success. His answer: great pizza. He knows that even the best surgeon in the world wouldn't get far without a crack team in the operating room, particularly first-rate nurses. So every month he orders pizza for the entire staff. In December he throws them a lavish holiday lunch. The rewards come back in spades. Nurses claw over one another to work with him, and he's the one surgeon who has no trouble getting overtime help.

> *Treat your staff well, and they'll march along with you.*

A little goes a long way. I'm always amazed at how much mileage you can get from a dozen doughnuts, a five-dollar box of chocolates, or letting an employee go home a half hour early once in a while. (I highly recommend Bob Nelson's book *1001 Ways to Reward Employees* as a source for additional ideas along these lines.)

4. Maintain the home front. Nurture and support employees' personal lives. No, I'm not suggesting that you run a dating service—just share the wealth a little and do what you can to make your employees' home and social lives

Put yourself in the shoes of whoever is unhappy or causing you trouble.

easier. Once in a while, spring for an inexpensive lunch. Plan an open house for employees, suppliers, even clients. Let your employees bring a spouse or a date to holiday parties; excluding significant others can generate animosity toward the company and stress in the home. When in doubt or under budget constraints, opt for less extravagant but no less inclusive celebrations.

5. Excel during adversity. It's easy to be a strong leader when everything's growing according to plan, but what do you do when the business environment hands you a lemon? Do you head for the door? Scream at your employees? Or do you roll up your sleeves? When handled properly, adversity can bring your team together in ways that winning never could.

For instance, suppose you've just learned that an employee stole from you or your biggest client took a walk. Here's how you should handle it:

- **Remain calm.** The entire company is watching you and will take its cues from your initial reaction. Keep a cool head.
- **Stall.** Whatever the bad news, you need time to craft an appropriate response. Make clear that you're troubled by the news and intend to make the matter your top priority. Then act.
- **Dig.** In all the crises I've faced, the bearer of the bad news rarely knew the whole story. If a client is bailing on your company, for example, find out exactly why. Perhaps the client is merely flexing his muscles over a disagreement with one of your employees and can still be saved. If not, you'll still need to explain the situation to your employees.
- **Analyze.** After you have all the facts, consider them from as many angles as possible. Put yourself in the shoes of whoever is unhappy or causing you trouble.
- **Plan.** Now develop a plan of action. Is the client truly thinking of leaving? Suppose you learn that this client

The Ten-Second Rule

Make it a practice to pause for ten long seconds before you react to new information, whether positive or negative—employee complaints, unhappy clients, potential big contracts, or anything else. This grace period helps ensure that your responses are well considered. It also trickles down to the employee, who may emulate your behavior and respect you for assessing the news carefully rather than flying off the handle.

Not long ago I was sitting in my office after a three-hour client negotiation, my head threatening to explode and my patience worn thin enough to see through. Suddenly, an employee burst in to announce that she had a brilliant idea: Turn off all the lights in the office for fifteen minutes twice a day. She thought it would be a great way to relieve stress; I thought it was a great way to make us the laughingstock of the industry. Still, I resisted the urge to reject her idea as ludicrous, and, most likely, offend her in the process. Instead, I left the room to compose myself— for a whole series of ten-second pauses. When I returned, she proceeded to elaborate on the theory behind her lights-out proposal. I politely suggested that as intriguing as her idea might be, we just couldn't risk losing thirty minutes of productivity a day, especially since we were growing like crazy and could barely handle things in the time available. Rather than leaving in a huff feeling berated or belittled, she saw my point and left feeling good about herself and her role in the company. She also appreciated having face time with the person in change.

ran roughshod over your employees. If you still need the business, then find a way for the client to save face without disciplining employees who may have done nothing wrong.

- **Execute.** After choosing a course of action, implement your plan. When you call the client back, be deferential. Let her know that you looked into the problem and removed the employee in question from the account. That will make the client feel valued.
- **Communicate.** Once you've decided what you're going to do, inform everyone who needs to know.

The Ten Commandments of Leadership Etiquette

Some of your toughest challenges as you grow will come from figuring out how to massage your relationship with your employees. As a leader, you hold the keys in many ways to your employees' dreams. What you might consider a mere business decision can affect not only their careers but also whether they can pay their bills and plan for their kids' education—and whether they feel good about coming to work or dread walking into the office every morning.

Every time you hold a meeting or send out a memo, imagine how your employees will interpret your words.

A sarcastic comment here, a blowup there, and the next thing you know, you have a demoralized, bitter, ineffective employee. The negativity will only multiply. So, every time you hold a meeting or send out a memo, imagine how your employees will interpret your words. Don't let your power so intoxicate you or your frustration so blind you that you forget how vulnerable almost everyone is to criticism or harsh words.

Likewise, don't be such a slave to your desire to be a beloved leader that you come across as too soft. I've always found that the most successful businesses have owners that are perceived as firm but fair.

Experience and observation have taught me, sometimes painfully, what I call the Ten Commandments of Leadership Etiquette:

1. Thou shalt not embarrass thine employees in front of others. Challenging an employee in public might make him want to quit before you're ready for that to happen. Instead, call the employee into your office and make your feelings known out of others' sight and hearing.

2. Thou shalt not cross boundaries. There's a fine line between being cordial and affable with your employees and being unprofessional or even self-sabotaging. It's great to go out with your staff occasionally, but if talk turns to work, leave. Be particularly vigilant at holiday parties, which often lead managers to let down their guard. Drink a bit too much, and you may irrevocably lose your employees' respect.

3. Thou shalt not accept gifts from suppliers. If you graciously refuse gifts from suppliers, you will not feel obligated to use their services and can implement the bidding process that will best suit your business. To avoid offending them, simply say your company policy forbids accepting gifts.

4. Thou shalt not air thy dirty laundry. Your employees do not need to hear about your problems, especially the personal ones. Using employees as counselors can make you appear weak or easily flustered.

5. Thou shalt not be petty. Let small things slide. If a normally reliable employee arrives a few minutes late to a meeting, let it pass. If you're out to lunch, pick up the tab or contribute more than your share; if your share is $8.00, throw in a twenty. You'll get a lot of mileage from those extra twelve bucks.

6. Thou shalt not flaunt thy success. Don't alienate your employees with lavish displays of your wealth. Envy is not a good motivator—unless you're motivating them to line up and demand raises.

7. Thou shalt not put thy people in compromising situations. Employees, like everyone else, are naturally curious. Don't leave important or sensitive documents lying around where someone might see them. Lock them up in a drawer, and lock your office at night.

8. Thou shalt not play favorites. Avoid having teacher's pets. Resist the urge to broadcast the names of your favorite employees or to pal around with them. Periodic praise is fine, but know that you risk making your other employees jealous, even hostile, toward the very people you want them to emulate.

9. Thou shalt not throw away power. Be careful of how much power you grant your employees. If you're giving someone a responsibility such as running your office, you're essentially giving her power over others. Is she really capable of acting appropriately and in accordance with your wishes?

10. Thou shalt not burn bridges. Sooner or later, one of your employees will quit. No matter how you feel, don't say anything you wouldn't want repeated. That's sound business practice, and, in any event, you may need this employee's help in showing the replacement the ropes. I've also had employees leave my company for their own reasons, only to call me three months later asking for their jobs back.

As with those other Ten Commandments, no one's perfect, but always *trying* to be a better leader is a necessary step toward developing an effective and harmonious organization where all employees stay focused and deliver on the same goal: growth.

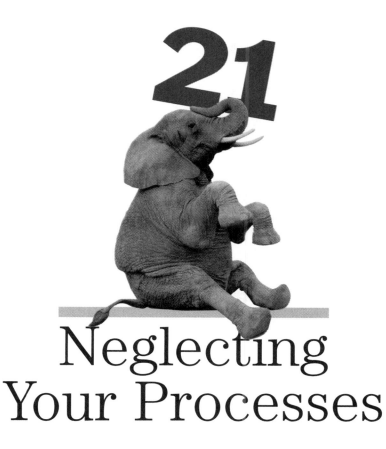

Neglecting
Your Processes

P rocesses? That's right. Procedures. Policies. Technical spec-
ifications. Documentation. You know, every important aspect
of your business and how it operates, written down so anybody
can follow them.

I know. You've got better things to do.

Well, actually, you don't. Not if you're growing and expect to come
out alive on the other side.

Few businesspeople are enamored of dealing with processes. It *can*
be tedious, especially for a creative genius like you. In fact, the trivial
details of processes are probably what drove you out the door and into
business for yourself in the first place. Right?

Well, if you neglect processes, if you expect them to run smoothly
on their own, they will inevitably come back to haunt you. You must
have adequate processes in place, ready to handle the increase in
business you want and expect to happen.

Just as keeping your body's processes working properly is the key
to maintaining your physical and mental health, designing and

maintaining good business processes brings multiple benefits for the health of your company. Well-thought-out processes enable you to manage growth and build the organization. They help you develop good employees, maintain product and service quality, and—not to be overlooked—get the best price for your company should you decide to sell it.

What Processes Are Good For

* Building the organization

* Developing people

* Managing growth

* Maintaining quality

* Maximizing company value

Even the smallest of businesses has many overlapping processes that interact. Think of your business for the moment as an automobile company. Assembling automobiles is just one of your processes; some others are acquiring raw materials, designing automobiles, marketing, and working your network of dealers.

Let's examine in more detail your assembly process. Right now you've got one assembly line, and that's fine for the business you're currently doing, but you're planning to sell three times as many cars next year. To triple your output, you can either make your one assembly line run three times as fast—which means more raw materials, new machinery, more efficiency, and so forth— or you can install additional assembly lines, for which you would also buy more raw materials and machinery, as well as hire more workers, and find more space. What's more, you've got to produce three times as many engines in another part of the plant (another process), and you have to handle three times as much paperwork as before and transport three times as many cars to dealers—and this just scratches the surface. If you fail to upgrade even one critical process, your entire business may struggle to keep up with the demands made on it. The money you invest in growth will be mostly wasted, and customers will begin drifting away because their cars are taking forever to get to them.

You don't make automobiles, you say? Your business is simpler? Maybe so, but the same principles apply. Whether you're making stationery, selling oranges, or tuning pianos, if you want to do more or different business, you have to plan for that growth, and that means building, examining, and upgrading all necessary processes—every single one of them.

If you fail to upgrade even one critical process, your entire business may struggle to keep up with the demands made on it.

If I were asked to identify the single most important reason why growing businesses crash, it would be the failure to create, develop, and implement the processes needed to handle that growth in the first place! You can't irrigate a thousand-acre bean field with a garden hose.

The Wheels Come Off

No matter the size of the business or the industry, companies whose processes aren't up to the job of handling growth typically find themselves on the path described below. See if any of it sounds familiar.

1. New customers come in, or existing customers spend more money with you, and your revenue begins to grow.

2. You find yourself and your employees pushing harder to fulfill the increase in business. (After all, your organization is small because you don't have the sales to support more employees.)

3. Your current customers are spending more, but they're also demanding more from you, and your customer service begins to suffer.

4. You notice that, although you're getting more business, there's still more opportunity out there and you're leaving too much money on the table. You could sell more if you only had the time and more good salespeople.

5. As problems multiply, you and your employees have to work harder and harder just putting out fires and staying afloat. Employee morale begins to sag.

6. You hire some help, but since you haven't upgraded your old processes or added new ones, your new employees can be used only as temporary patches or for crisis management.

7. Communication within and between departments deteriorates. No one has time to talk.

8. The workload becomes overwhelming.

9. Unable to deliver what your customers want, you begin losing big clients, key employees leave, and you're in worse shape than you were before you grew.

The time to put processes in place is, of course, before you need them.

This path of self-destruction can be avoided if you take the time *up front* to put in place the processes needed to handle the growth. Processes are the foundation of your business; you can't expect the processes of a smaller business to support the larger structure your business is becoming.

The time to put processes in place is, of course, before you need them. Failure to prepare for growth can put you face-to-face with any or all of these unpleasant scenarios:

Explosion. It's inevitable in many cases: There isn't enough capacity to handle the demand, and the organization simply blows up. Think of each of your old processes, the way you do things now, as a pipeline that gets weaker and weaker as too much is pushed through it; eventually, something's got to give.

Stunting. Even if you can deliver on your current commitments to your customers and survive by patching your pipeline, you won't be able to do so for long—and, more important, you're pretty much maxed out, growth-wise.

Stress. No one wants to work day after day in a stressful environment, but that's what you're asking your employees to do by not giving them an effective way to accomplish their work.

Defection. Enough is enough for even the most loyal employees. Incentives and retention strategies can help, but they'll fall short if the organization itself is inefficient.

Involuntary servitude. A successful business owner is usually, by choice, a prisoner of his work. But that's different from being chained to your desk because the company would fall apart without you.

Fumble!

Football fanatics Sam Jones and Butch Sims were friends who had played ball together at the same college. They had not been quite good enough to make it as pros, though, and several years later they found themselves teaching at different elementary schools—and missing the gridiron.

They missed it so much that they decided to get back in the game. Using their connections with some professional football players, a local college's playing field, and some canny advertising, they opened Gridiron Glory, a summer football camp for elementary school kids. The chance to learn the fundamentals and finer points of the game from the pros attracted 100 kids to the first session. Campers were assigned equipment and uniforms at check-in and stayed for five days of top-notch football instruction.

Sam and Butch were living their dream: playing football and making money. Things went so well the first summer that they decided to make the second year an even bigger success by adding two more five-day sessions and increasing the number of campers per session to 350. As soon as word of mouth got out, deposits began flooding in. Soon there were 1,050 registrants eager to play ball.

The disaster began at check-in for the first week's session. The lines stretched out, and so did the wait, which soon grew to two hours. Then 350 ravenous kids and their angry parents marched on the cafeteria, where food quickly ran out and another two hours elapsed while overwhelmed staff frantically searched for more. They were already in panic mode before the afternoon training session started. Again, long lines formed for each drill, with fidgety, hyperenergetic kids spending more time in line than in practice.

The remainder of the first five-day session was a nightmare. Between answering calls from irate parents, all Sam and Butch could do was put out a few of the hottest fires. Word of mouth, which had helped make the first year's camp such a success, now came back to bite them; nearly 15 percent of registrants for the two remaining sessions canceled.

It didn't take a rocket scientist to see what the problem was. Gridiron lacked processes to handle the growing stream of campers: a registration process to handle the first morning's flood of kids and parents, a cafeteria process to feed the expected increase in hungry campers, a training process to keep kids moving from one exercise to another without long waits in line.

Unfortunately, the importance of processes didn't dawn on our football heroes until it was too late. They assumed that the same procedures they had used so successfully the first year would be enough to handle more than three times that flow rate the next. The results were disappointed kids, angry parents, and an ignominious end for Gridiron Glory.

Five Steps to Better Processes

Now let's turn to the meat and potatoes: my five-step program for successful process building. What follows is an example—Argosy Audio & Video theater and component store—that will guide you and your team as you analyze each step of your business processes.

Step 1: Create an overview map of a central or key process of your company, outlining in general what the company must do from the beginning through the end of the process. Be sure to include every function. I find it easiest to begin with the last step. For instance, in a retail or service operation, start with the delivery of the product or service to the customer; then work upstream through the process, all the way back to meeting the prospective customer.

Argosy's process flow begins with the prospect and ends (if successful) with a satisfied customer. The process that makes this happen includes greeting the prospect, making the sale, completing the

Brand the Effort

I've found that naming the action of reconfiguring or creating processes improves employee buy-in. Even a simple name like "Growing Smart" or "SuccessNext" will do the job. Communicate the effort on posters; update employees regularly with e-mail, notes, and memos. When you're ready to kick off the change, have a company lunch and honor those who have played key roles in the planning. Your employees will feel pride in working for a smart, growing company. Expect an immediate improvement in morale.

purchase transaction, getting the product into the customer's hands (at the store or by delivery), and following through to ensure customer satisfaction.

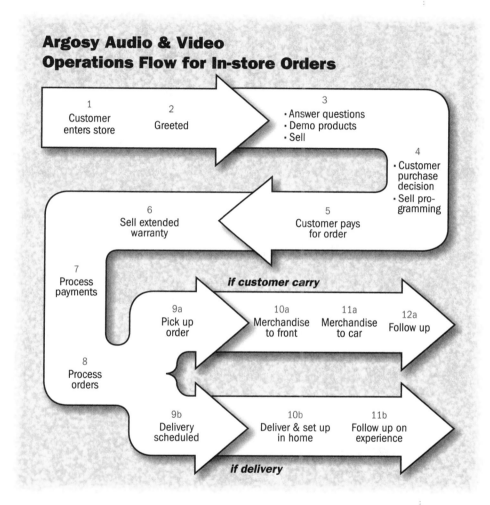

Argosy Audio & Video
Operations Flow for In-store Orders

1
Customer enters store

2
Greeted

3
• Answer questions
• Demo products
• Sell

4
• Customer purchase decision
• Sell pro-gramming

6
Sell extended warranty

5
Customer pays for order

7
Process payments

if customer carry

9a
Pick up order

10a
Merchandise to front

11a
Merchandise to car

12a
Follow up

8
Process orders

9b
Delivery scheduled

10b
Deliver & set up in home

11b
Follow up on experience

if delivery

Step 2: Go through each step on the process map and chart out the actions required to complete that step. Some of the steps may seem to be no-brainers, but if they are essential parts of the process, write them down. You'll need to identify even the most trivial steps in order to make the whole process more efficient. For example, step 10a in Argosy's process, "Merchandise to front," seems elementary, but if you begin to examine the details of the action and its place in the overall flow, you may discover that there's a more efficient way to arrange your inventory, move boxes into or out of the warehouse, or direct the customer's vehicle to get the job done. That's why even the simplest steps should be mapped.

Step 3: Look for ways to combine tasks for higher efficiency. Assign or reapportion each task to an appropriate department (as shown in the Argosy example), or have the responsible department redesign the task to enhance functionality or save time or expense. Not every action needs its own separate department; remember, you want to combine tasks for efficiency. Improved process efficiency will show up as greater operational effectiveness, improved customer satisfaction, and a gain in profitability.

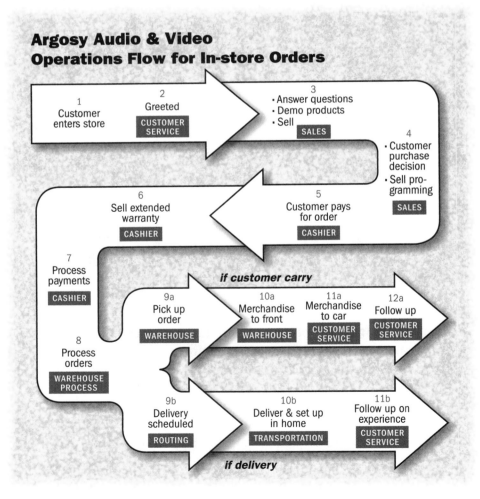

Argosy Audio & Video
Operations Flow for In-store Orders

1 Customer enters store

2 Greeted — CUSTOMER SERVICE

3
- Answer questions
- Demo products
- Sell — SALES

4
- Customer purchase decision
- Sell programming — SALES

5 Customer pays for order — CASHIER

6 Sell extended warranty — CASHIER

7 Process payments — CASHIER

8 Process orders — WAREHOUSE PROCESS

if customer carry

9a Pick up order — WAREHOUSE

10a Merchandise to front — WAREHOUSE

11a Merchandise to car — CUSTOMER SERVICE

12a Follow up — CUSTOMER SERVICE

9b Delivery scheduled — ROUTING

10b Deliver & set up in home — TRANSPORTATION

11b Follow up on experience — CUSTOMER SERVICE

if delivery

Look at each department to determine how the whole picture can be reshaped more effectively. For example, steps 3 and 4 in Argosy's process map require salespeople to answer questions, demonstrate products, and sell programming to prospects. Argosy must determine how many salespeople it needs to meet the revenue projections.

Step 9b, on the other hand, requires Argosy to develop a shipping-and-logistics function to schedule deliveries. This task can be accomplished either internally—by hiring staff—or by outsourcing to a shipping company. Either way, staff will be required to coordinate the activity, and a flow step will need to be developed for that function.

Improved process efficiency will show up as greater operational effectiveness, improved customer satisfaction, and a gain in profitability.

Step 4: Reexamine your processes in light of your growth expectations—and multiply throughput (such as orders and sales) by three, just to be safe. Ask yourself the following questions as they relate to the increase in volume:

- Where will the bottlenecks occur?
- How do I eliminate these bottlenecks?
- Which departments will be responsible for maintaining the quality of product and service?
- Do I need new departments to handle any new facets of the business?
- How can I increase the capacity or efficiency of each step in the process?

Step 5: Create your "new" process map. Incorporate the information from the first four steps to design your new work flow. Don't think about current personnel or functions at this stage; if you do, you'll wind up with the same bottlenecks.

Companies hire high-priced consultants to set up processes and sometimes program them into computer systems. I've paid big, seven-figure money to such consultants, but I've found

How Much to Process?

It's important to create processes before you find yourself in crisis mode—but how many processes, and how detailed? If you're a small, five-person, quick-print brokerage selling only printing, your processes obviously won't need to be as numerous or detailed as if you were a huge, 300-person, full-service printing company. Here's a good rule of thumb: Reexamine your growth projections, assume the results will be three times as good as you expect, and build processes to handle that level of business. This gives you a 3X safety factor against the hazards of growth. Caution: Don't run out and hire people just yet, but have your upgraded processes and work flow ready to implement when the need arises.

that in many cases the owner and employees can do it faster, better, and cheaper. Just tap into the know-how of your key people.

Beware, however, of the key employee, usually on the operations side, that you "can't live without." This is the person whose hands are in everything; she's found in many businesses. Relying entirely on such a person is a clear sign that you need better processes—written policy and procedures that can be followed by anybody. What happens if this key person falls ill, or quits, or demands the moon at her next employee review? You're in hot water, that's what.

Be aware also that some team members may resist change. Even though process changes might help them do their work more efficiently, employees often fear that any change would mean for them a loss of power or influence in the company. Reassure them that this is not the case. Once you've developed your new process flow, you can assign the right person to each function. Your employees will then be more productive—and happier.

Corrupting
the Culture

B ob Claremont and Brett Moore are co-owners and partners in the Spectra Design Group, a seven-person firm specializing in architecture and interior design. Spectra's customers are high-net-worth individuals who hire them to design and decorate single-family custom homes. The company does great work and gets most of its customers through referrals.

The two developed a horizontal growth strategy, getting new types of customers to buy their existing services. They expanded their target market to include developers of high-end communities built around golf courses. The positioning made perfect sense. The houses started around $1 million; the typical buyer was older, experienced in working with designers, and wealthy enough to afford Spectra's high rates.

Spectra planned to sell its services in bulk at a slight discount to the developers, who would then mark it up and sell it to their home buyers. They hit it big almost immediately, landing the first three developers they pitched, and their business and life changed instantly. Instead of working on a handful of projects, they found themselves juggling twenty to twenty-five projects at a time.

Luckily they had thought ahead and planned for the increased volume (no doubt they read the previous chapter). For each of their operational steps, from creative through design, layout, and even billing, they implemented processes that enabled them to handle rapid growth. The windfall of income allowed them to hire thirty more employees, many of whom had substantial experience that enhanced Spectra's capabilities and corporate image. Life was great for Bob and Brett.

The key is to acknowledge that your culture *will* change, get out in front of it, and lead the organization through a smooth transition.

Sounds like a dream, right? Well, the dream turned into a nightmare and monsters started coming out from under the bed. Many of the employees who had been there from the beginning began to feel unappreciated, and resentful of the new, higher-level hires. They felt they had been responsible for the success of the company and that these new hires were reaping all the benefits— collecting large salaries and taking all the leadership positions.

Bob and Brett, preoccupied with managing the huge increase in business, didn't pay much attention to the complaints. Then things got truly ugly. Infighting and turf wars became the norm. Even the simplest tasks didn't get done; four employees quit in frustration, leaving Spectra critically understaffed in vital areas.

A de facto hierarchy arose; senior management no longer associated with rank and file. The company's culture changed from that of a family, in which people knew each other, worked together, and hung out after work, to a sterile, factorylike minibureaucracy.

Spectra's experience is not uncommon; in fact, it's almost inevitable that the culture will change when the company grows. Adding employees or processes to your current business changes the way things are done. The more new employees, new personalities, and new processes, the bigger the potential for a shift in culture. If it's managed properly, growth can improve the environment; if not, it can corrupt the culture.

How do you keep growth from corrupting the culture and laying waste to your esprit de corps? First, by being aware of the danger. The key is to acknowledge that your culture *will* change, get out in front of it, and lead the organization through a smooth transition. Don't get blindsided, or else you'll end up conducting damage control—a very precarious position to be in.

Smoothing Out the Bumps

When I was growing my businesses, I knew people were constantly assessing my attitudes and actions: How would I handle the success? Would I share the credit? Would I look out for the employees who had been with me from the early days, who stayed loyal to the company during the lean times?

Over the years and for many businesses, I've developed a list of measures to take to ensure that a company's culture will evolve smoothly and make a successful transition to greater growth. As you read these, you might say to yourself, *Hey, I don't have to do this—after all, it's my company.* Yes, I would answer, it *is* your company, but wouldn't you rather take a few inexpensive precautions now than have to deal with a lot of costly aggravation later?

1. Respect the microscope. Recognize that, to your employees, you will be like a bug under a microscope. Your every move will be analyzed, and the more success your company achieves, the more intense the scrutiny. Accepting this simple but inevitable fact will help you avoid some of the more petty but dangerous problems.

Culture Change Made Easy

1. Respect the microscope.

2. Share the spotlight.

3. Involve others in shaping the business.

4. Promote from within.

5. Communicate effectively.

The way to keep people happy to work for you is to respect them and treat them as people. A little humility, at times, also helps. This will reassure your veterans that they are still important to you, and it will tell your new hires that they too are important to the company. It will foster an atmosphere of openness, communication, and flexibility that will encourage employee commitment and ownership rather than bureaucratic rigidity.

How do you keep the atmosphere friendly and open?

> **I've never wanted to be a rock star—just to build and run a business that rocks and rolls.**

- **Spend time with the rank and file.** I always said hello to people I passed on the way to my office. This sets a good tone and a good example for every manager in the workplace.
- **Don't shut out the old regime.** Your longtime employees will feel privileged to have a special link to the guy at the top. This is a useful tool for maintaining employee morale—as well as getting inside information. Don't waste it.
- **Keep track of employees' key personal dates.** I had my secretary create a running list for me of birthdays and other important dates, so I could personally acknowledge them.
- **Be social.** Stop by cubicles, offices, and the loading dock to say hello. Join the office football pool. Sit down at the break table now and then. You'll be surprised at how much you can learn about your company from your frontline employees—things that your managers may be reluctant to bring up.
- **Let's do lunch.** If possible, every week or two, order a pizza or sandwiches for the troops. Invite everybody— management as well as rank and file—to the lunch. This fosters social interaction between management and everyone else, and it will go far in boosting productivity.

2. Share the spotlight. I've never wanted to be a rock star—just to build and run a business that rocks and rolls. My objective is big profits, and I'm happy to give the credit, accolades, and attention to the people who do the work that it takes to make my businesses a huge success. Never forget that no matter how good you are, you cannot do it by yourself. Even when I was making 90 percent of the sales for my $30 million, ten-person marketing firm, I wasn't alone. I had operations and administrative people, without whom I wouldn't have been able to execute the sales I had made. Whenever I received praise in a discussion or an interview, I always made it a point to acknowledge someone else in the company. I believe in giving credit where credit is due—and you can't imagine how that builds loyalty.

At weekly lunch meetings, I reviewed the week's positives and praised several people for the good work they had done. With the help of an assistant, I kept track of names I had mentioned so I could find new people to praise each week to reinforce outstanding performance. It was true for my company, and it's true for you: Worker satisfaction shows up at the bottom line.

Your best employees want to believe they're making a difference in the company and that their hard work will be noticed and rewarded through career advancement. This is why a formal award for outstanding performance, presented in front of a public or company audience, both rewards and motivates them.

I once created a reward-and-information-sharing system that I called the Knowledge Program. It was designed to give all my employees, in all departments and all countries, access to key employees whose knowledge of particular subjects was critical to the success of my business. I listed ten crucial areas—including sales, shipping, market research, and production—then established criteria for measuring contributions to each of them. My division presidents nominated star employees in their departments. Judges (senior management and I) selected the winners and crowned the company's Knowledge Leader in each category. Besides the accolades, these experts each received a

Worker satisfaction shows up at the bottom line.

nice dinner and a plaque. We also distributed booklets picturing the recipients and highlighting their accomplishments. From that time on, other employees sought out these ordained experts to answer questions, adding to their prestige within the company.

The program was a smashing success and created a huge buzz. It even won a Mercury Award for Outstanding Achievement in Professional Communications, an international competition held by MerComm, Inc. Productivity grew—not only that of the Knowledge Leaders, who had newfound esteem and motivation, but of other employees as well, who now knew whom to approach with their questions.

> **Rewarding such deserving but unsung people not only reinforces hard work and loyalty, but it also improves morale throughout the company.**

Rewarding star performers is important, but it does not follow that less flashy achievers should be ignored. Don't neglect the amiable, hard-working but unassuming lower-level worker, who is often cheered on by his colleagues but perhaps overlooked by managers and executives. Reward such employees with new responsibilities, a well-timed promotion, or generous praise during a company meeting. Show that you recognize and appreciate a solid work ethic, regardless of employee rank. Make it a point to spend a little time talking with them in the halls or at their desks. Others will see that you consider them valuable employees and will emulate their behavior. Rewarding such deserving but unsung people not only reinforces hard work and loyalty, it also improves morale throughout the company. After all, your lower-level employees are the building blocks of your operations.

3. Involve others in shaping the business. Implementing new policies and procedures changes the way many of your employees will have to perform their jobs—but everyone likes to have a say in her future. As you plan for expansion, include your best, most productive, most dedicated people in your discussions. They will have valuable perspective on their roles and will appreciate the fact that you value their opinion; and they will actively help make the changes necessary for growth and will lead and inspire others to do likewise.

This doesn't mean you have to agree with everything your employees suggest; in the end, the company is your responsibility, and you have to exercise your own judgment. But you should at least involve them in gathering information and suggesting new policies to handle the growth of the business. You might find, as I did, that they rise to the occasion. At the very least you'll get better compliance.

4. Promote from within. Nothing sends a better message. When the time comes to put capable people in charge of important tasks or new departments, look first at those who were with you when you began growing. Even if they haven't run departments or managed other employees, their company experience and insights may make them your best candidates overall. Promoting from within saves time and money, and because the promoted employee knows the business, she is not likely to require much training to do an excellent job right out of the gate. Some of my best managers were employees who started part time and worked their way up.

Be careful, however, to match your employees with the positions they're best suited for. When you're growing, this can be natural; you'll have many new needs and roles to fill. As your company grows, ask your most productive and visionary employees to submit plans to grow their departments. Review the plans and, based on their merit, put those employees first in line to be in charge of the effort. Look at growth as an opportunity to shift people to better-fitting roles.

> When the time comes to put capable people in charge of important tasks or new departments, look first at those who were with you when you began growing.

I once had an administrative assistant named Joan. By any measure, Joan was a bad assistant—so bad that I would end up doing a lot of her work as well as my own. But she was pleasant, outgoing, loved by all, and devoted to the company—a model employee in all respects but performance. I didn't want to lose her, but how could I keep her?

I was in the process of implementing a growth strategy that included selling our services to new target markets. Suddenly it hit me—maybe Joan would fit this sales role. We sat down and had a heart-to-heart. She admitted she hated administrative work and had no aptitude for it. What she really liked to do was sell.

I slept on it and decided to give her a chance. I assigned her a few of the new targeted accounts. Sure enough, Joan made some headway and turned into an excellent salesperson. In the end, she had a new career and I had another good seller. She always remained grateful that I gave her a second chance, and she became one of my most loyal employees.

When filling new roles needed for growth, evaluate your employees carefully, especially those who underperform. Look at their strengths and weaknesses. Distinguish employees who lack effort and capability from underperformers with great potential and, if possible, make an adjustment. Today's poor traffic manager might be tomorrow's great telemarketer.

Look at growth as an opportunity to shift people to better-fitting roles.

Be careful, though. Promote people to a better fit, not merely as a reward. A different problem can arise with employees who are so good at what they do that they win a promotion to a different job—and fail. A salesperson, for example, may make a lousy sales manager; the drive, the desire to work alone, and other skills that make him successful in one position can work against him in other jobs.

5. Communicate effectively. This one's a must. If you don't keep your employees in the loop, they will imagine the worst. Communicate successes with the whole team—new customers, sales records, industry reviews. If there's bad news coming, let it come from you and not through the grapevine. Your employees need to know you're playing straight with them.

Although it can be difficult to keep up with the pace of events, tell employees about changes in the organization before they happen. Think through all aspects of these changes and how they will affect the people in the room. For example, hiring more salespeople will obviously have a direct impact on the current sales force, so make sure you communicate how the territories or accounts will work, the effects on the commission structure, and other issues that will directly affect sales staff. Think about how expanding the sales staff will affect the rest of the company—customer service, account management, and other departments. Put yourself in the position of every person or department in the company, anticipate every possible issue, then address those concerns.

> **If there's bad news coming, let it come from you and not through the grapevine. Your employees need to know you're playing straight with them.**

If substantial hiring, layoffs, or restructuring is in the cards, first finish your planning, then promptly inform employees in full so they can digest the news and get back to work. A plan that keeps changing will distract and disturb employees, and morale and productivity will suffer.

Rely on your most respected and influential employees— not necessarily supervisors only. Explain the plan to them in advance, share your thinking about implementation, and enlist their support in communicating the changes to others. Then, after your meeting with the entire company, you will have people in place to back and champion the plan.

Implementing growth reaches its critical stage when your plans go into the hands of your employees. This is a delicate and vulnerable time for both your company and the individuals who make it work. Take care to have all the bases covered, and as many lieutenants as possible on board for the effort, before you enter this phase. If you do, you'll have your best shot at making your chosen growth strategy a roaring success.

You're Ready!

If you've read this far, and thought about what you've read, and especially if you've started putting theory into practice by working the numbers, you now know what it takes to increase the size and profitability of your business with minimal risk. You know how to analyze your business model and determine whether it's in good condition and ready to handle rapid, massive growth. You're ready to engage your sales force in searching out growth opportunities and securing customer commitments to realize them. You're prepared to evaluate these opportunities, their upsides and their downsides, and choose the one or two that are most likely to lead to success.

You've gained insights into maximizing the value of your products, your services, and your business as a whole. You understand that growth requires processes that allow you to execute on all facets of your new, bigger business. And you've just finished reading some cautionary tales about mistakes and missteps you can and should avoid.

Now you're ready for the fun part—growing your business. Go forth and Be the Elephant!

The Difference
Maker Inc.

W hat is The Difference Maker Inc.? It's something I wish I had had when I was building my businesses. When I was starting out, I had no time to join "presidents groups." And since I was the one in charge, I had no one to kick around ideas with. Family and friends, however supportive, lacked the knowledge and experience to provide any meaningful advice. Books targeting businesses didn't really focus on the key issues that confronted me. I hungered for guidance from people I could trust, advice about proven strategies and tactics that I could implement to make an immediate difference in my business. But no one ever took a stance and said "Do this" or "Do that." I had to learn on my own, by trial and error.

That's why I created The Difference Maker Inc., a business that fills that void for those who wish to pursue success by following in my footsteps. It does so by providing the advice, leadership, and practical know-how that I couldn't find. (Go to **www.differencemaker.com.**)

I've structured the service lines of The Difference Maker Inc. around the factors that have the greatest impact on business success. If you can succeed in these facets of business, you're well on your way to big-time success!

Rock Solid! Your Business on Solid Footing. This category of service focuses on the areas critical to success from the planning and business architecture perspective, with the objective of generating the best business model possible. Issues featured include: (1) business models, (2) projections, (3) generating assumptions, (4) using projections to shape your business, (5) assessing risks, (6) statements you really need, and (7) business viability and assessment.

Bag the Elephant: Getting Big Customers. This service line focuses on how to get the big customer, the one that can change your life. It includes: (1) positioning your business for the Elephant, (2) five things to know about big companies, (3) embracing bureaucracy, (4) finding your ideal prospects, (5) knocking on doors, (6) meeting your prospects, (7) picking champions, (8) building alliances, and (9) deadly perils to avoid in Elephant Land.

Be the Elephant: Growth and Value Strategies. This service line details my method for expanding a business and maximizing its value. Included are: (1) my ten steps to business expansion, (2) white space analysis, (3) growth strategy options, (4) assessing viability, (5) operations outlook, (6) why customers really buy, (7) creating value, (8) USPs and more.

Squeeze the Tube: Getting the Most from Your Employees. Business owners typically credit much of their success—or failure—to their employees. I've found that the biggest concern for business owners is how to identify and retain good employees and maximize their potential. This service line focuses on: (1) the three indispensable human elements I've most often encountered, (2) eight principles of leadership, (3) motivation, (4) the pyramid of salespeople's needs, (5) managing your salespeople, (6) value sales quotient, and (7) performers versus nonperformers.

Just Desserts! Selling Your Business. This service line tells exactly what is needed to get your business and yourself ready for a potential sale, what to expect during the sale, and how to prepare for life thereafter. Included are: (1) understanding and mastering deal structures, (2) the closing process, (3) developing a platform for negotiations, (4) hiring the right representative to get the most from your sales, and (5) demonstrating the due diligence purchasers are looking for.

At **www.differencemaker.com,** you can learn more about the service lines, as well as these other products and services:

Business Boost free e-newsletter.
This is a high-quality, thought-provoking source for actionable tips, advice, and real-world success stories straight from the trenches, in all disciplines. You'll get big-customer tactics from the Bag the Elephant line, strategies to grow your business from the Be the Elephant line, plus some of the best resources around. This newsletter will help you define yourself as a leader, shape your business for success, even increase the sale value of your business—and it's free!

The Difference Maker Workshops.
These are intensive three-day programs focusing on issues most critical to the business. Each workshop includes material from each service line, with break-out sessions to address and analyze attendees' specific issues.

Toolboxes with Power Tools.
This is a partner and resource I really wish I had had: fifteen years of experience rolled into simple, effective, step-by-step strategies and tactics to help your business succeed, available at the click of a mouse. The Power Tools are proprietary detailed charts, templates, and worksheets that facilitate your use of the toolbox material in your own business.

Steve—One-on-One.
This individual program is tailored to meet the specific needs of your business. Whether it's working with your management on organizational issues, training your team to get that BIG customer, developing successful growth strategies to expand your business, or that keynote address at your annual meeting, these sessions will have a major impact.

About the Author

Steve Kaplan has made a career of shepherding businesses to success and helping others do the same. Turning Sampling Corporation of America (SCA), a basement operation, into a $250 million, 1,300-employee marketing company spanning sixteen countries was only the beginning. Over the past twenty years, he has helped more than one hundred businesses of all sizes and industries get big customers, restructure themselves, improve efficiency, boost morale, expand into new markets, and evaluate exit strategies, among other things. Recently he has been the managing partner in a venture specializing in providing equity and operating strategy to a range of businesses.

As an expert entrepreneur, Steve has been recognized by *Inc.* magazine as a finalist for Entrepreneur of the Year and has won the Mercury Excellence Award in Employee Motivation. He has been the subject of many print interviews and profiles at home and abroad in such media as *Advertising Age, Crain's Business, Food &*

Beverage, Selling, Target Marketing, and the *Chicago Tribune.* His business practices have been featured in several college textbooks.

A graduate of Bradley University in Peoria, Illinois, Steve received his MBA from Rosary Graduate School of Business in River Forest, Illinois. He has taught courses in advertising, marketing, and business organization at Triton College in River Grove, Illinois. He is a sought-after public speaker, presenting keynote speeches and workshops for businesses of all sizes on many business topics. He has appeared on a variety of media (including CBS, NBC, and Fox Television) to discuss his experiences and insights. He has also written articles for business magazines such as *Target Marketing.* He is a *New York Times, Wall Street Journal, Business Week,* and *USA Today* bestselling author.

Steve's vision and leadership made BountySCA Worldwide one of the world's leading marketing-service, database, and media organizations. He was a member of the executive committee of Euro RSCG, a 176-company conglomerate, and is the founder of The Difference Maker Inc., a company providing packaged tools and advice across a variety of business disciplines. He is also the owner of the investment firm Kaplan Enterprises LLC and a partner in eSkape, a 60,000-square-foot Chicago-area family entertainment center.

Steve chairs the Kaplan Family Foundation, a private foundation dedicated to the advancement of entrepreneurship in the youth of today.

Steve believes that both business *and* life should be an adventure and that both should be pursued with passion and vigor. Some of the adventures Steve has been fortunate to experience include: scuba diving with hammerhead sharks in the Galapagos Islands and whale sharks in the Chale Islands, Africa; running with the bulls in Pamplona, Spain; ski paragliding in Verbier, France; bungee jumping; gorilla trekking in the Congo; whitewater rafting; hot air ballooning over the Masa Mara, Africa; and body rafting in New Zealand.

Acknowledgments

I'd like to thank the following people, without whose help and support *Be the Elephant* would never have been. Many of you were with me for my first book, so double thanks to you.

Thanks, Jim Levine. You're more than a literary agent; your advice was right on the money, every step of the way.

Thank you, Jeff Morris, for your technical expertise and creative flair. I said in the last book that I couldn't even think of writing another one without you—and I didn't, so thanks for the great effort again on this book.

Thanks to J. J. for your creative inspiration, style, and advice, plus the great work from Descubrir.

Thank you, Peter Workman. The first time we met in your office, I knew that Workman Publishing was the right place for this book.

Thank you, Richard Rosen. Your ideas, editing, and sense of humor made this a great experience.

Thank you, Team Workman, from creative to photography, design, editing, marketing, publicity, selling, and everything in between, it's been a pleasure working with such first-class people: Brian Belfiglio, Andrea Fleck, Paul Gamarello, Leora Kahn, Ron Longe, Jen Paré, Dove Pedlosky, Amanda Pritzker, Kristy Ramsammy, and Carol White.

Thanks to David Hahn and everyone at Planned Television Arts for their effort and hard work in making this book a success: Jared Sharpe, Virginia Quiambao, and Dennelle Catlett.

And thanks, finally, to Karen the elephant, courtesy of R. W. Commerford & Sons, Goshen, CT.

Index